BAMBO JORDAN

BAMBO JORDAN

An Anthropological Narrative

Bruce T. Williams

WAVELAND

PRESS, INC.

Prospect Heights, Illinois

For information about this book, write or call:

Waveland Press, Inc.
P.O. Box 400
Prospect Heights, Illinois 60070
(708) 634-0081

TO CLAIRE

For coming and sharing
Bambo Jordan with me—
and so much more.

Contents

Top: *Jordan Dama, 1965.* Bottom: *Robert, Lester, and Jordan at the Ntcheu market, 1965.*

Introduction

Jordan Dama is a cook and a peasant farmer. He lives with his wife, Ida, and several of his many children in Magola village near Mphephozinai in the Ntcheu District of Malawi in southern Africa. At the time of this writing, Jordan is working as a cook for a South African diplomat in Lilongwe, the capital city of Malawi. He is about sixty years old.

I came to know Jordan in September, 1964, when as Peace Corps volunteers, I and a friend hired him to be our cook. He worked for us for twenty-one months, and after my departure he continued his employment with some new volunteers who replaced me and my partner. In 1972, I was in Malawi again to begin work on a Ph.D. dissertation, and Jordan and I spent some time together. Unfortunately, a number of serious political problems within Malawi led to a situation whereby I could not carry out the research, and so I was forced to leave. In 1980, I served as the first Director of the Centre for Social Research at the University of Malawi in Zomba, where we conducted project evaluations for development agencies as well as doing original social and economic research. Jordan came to work for me and my wife, Claire, and our two children, and we employed him this time for two years. Through letters we have been in regular contact during the intervals between those two periods of employment and from 1982 to the present. I have known Jordan for almost thirty years.

The word *Bambo* in the book's title simply means father, or somewhat as English speakers say sir or mister, and is used frequently among Malawians when men are addressed. Sometimes

1

it is attached to a name, as in Bambo Jordan, and sometimes it is just used alone. It is an expression of respect.

The Republic of Malawi is a small landlocked country on the southern edge of the Rift Valley in east-central Africa. Approximately the size of Pennsylvania, it has a population of about 9 million people, which includes five major and six smaller ethnic groups, each with its own language.

Dependent on sales of tobacco, tea, sugar, and groundnuts for its income, Malawi does a creditable job economically and has succeeded in feeding its citizens. Expenditures for education and health services have remained small, however, as the government has directed investment into large, privately owned farms or estates and into exported cash crops. This strategy has come at considerable cost to the small holder or peasant farmer who survives on increasingly overcrowded and soil-depleted land. While politically stable since its independence from Britain in July 1964, before which it was known as Nyasaland, Malawi has recently shown some significant signs of internal criticism directed toward the life president, Dr. H. Kamuzu Banda, the only indigenous leader the country has known. Today, there is a call for a multiparty political system, and this poses a serious challenge to the Malawi Congress Party and the elderly president.

Malawi is an extremely beautiful country with an unparalleled variety of terrain—high, cool, steep-sided plateaux; rich alluvial farm lands; numerous mountains covered with cedar and pine forests, one of three thousand meters; a tropical lowland; and a lake six hundred kilometers long—all within a small area. (I have never lived in the country as a tourist, only as a Peace Corps volunteer or as a working anthropologist. But it would be foolish not to acknowledge Malawi's offerings to travelers.)

This book is neither a history nor an ethnography, but rather a part of a relatively new genre of works that are often called narrative ethnographies. Unlike many of the stodgy monographs I read as an undergraduate years ago, narrative ethnographies use an imaginative effort to keep the stories lively and impassioned through a style of writing and format of presentation that can evoke a reader response, both hearty and tender. I have called *Bambo Jordan* an anthropological narrative simply to emphasize its story-like qualities, and also because the presentation relies so heavily on dialogue as novels do as well, to reveal the characters.

The effort to label this book may seem like folly, best left to book editors and professors of literary form, but anthropologists are actually waging quite an important debate over the issue of how fieldwork observations should be presented. Describing events is quite difficult for many reasons and chief among them is the fact that observers see things differently. We have all had the confusing experience of hearing two different versions of the same event which had been shared by two participants. And what of the professionally trained anthropologist who enters into a new culture? Human beings are surely far from the point where we are without biases and values that will influence our ways of seeing the world, and so should we not always be suspicious when a claim has been made that a reporter has put biases aside in getting to the truth?

For much of the first half of the twentieth century, leaders in the study of anthropology moved to make the discipline an increasingly scientific and factual enterprise. In part, this movement was a reaction against missionaries and colonials and adventurers who described "natives" in a casual or haphazard and often unflattering and insensitive way. The move to establish anthropology as a science, thereby making the anthropologists scientific experts with dominion over the "other," was accomplished in large measure by insisting on improved fieldwork methods, which generally demanded intense, difficult, and lengthy participant-observation research. But once endured, it was the fieldwork that gave the anthropologist a claim on the truth.

Interestingly, the writings of these earlier observer scientists were unemotional and detached and written in the third person, and this dispassionate presentation masked the highly complex involvement of the anthropologist with those observed. This was a curious situation. The effort to become more objective and scientific required more comprehensive and sophisticated fieldwork techniques, thereby compelling the anthropologist to have an even more passionate and empathic relation among those with whom he lived. But the presentation often remained sterile, lifeless, and distant. And, the fieldwork experience, the place where the actual social interaction and communication took place, was hidden from view; and one was left to wonder how the anthropologist came to know things.

In the late 1960s and early 1970s a major transition began to take place in the United States, probably as a result of the social turbulence of the sixties, a time of suspicion of authority and experts, whether parental, political, or scholarly. Seemingly in response, the discipline of anthropology opened itself up for inspection in the sense that a large number of works was published which dealt with the fieldwork experience. These were important writings because they began to examine what this research process, based as it was on an intense fieldwork experience, was all about;

and these works focused on the anthropologist, who became the acknowledged critical link between those studied and what would be written.

Recent critics of these works argue that the writings, while useful, were often so introspective and self-indulgent that they almost became the fieldworkers' confessions, practically overlooking the people studied. More importantly, they failed to reveal the two-sided process that takes place when the researcher and the people meet and interact. So we learned a good deal about the anthropologists, but not enough about the process of how people came to know one another.

Recently the attempt has been made to achieve a more balanced exploration of this place of interaction—the *point of dialogue*, as some have called it—where the anthropologist learns and does anthropology and where we can see the process revealed in the actual incidents, interpretations, and communications of the participants themselves. There is, then, a conscious attempt to clearly place the anthropologist in the research itself, because the anthropologist mediates the process of discovery.

Some anthropologists have chosen to pursue this complex subject theoretically, and this is proper. In *Bambo Jordan*, I have chosen to continue with the new genre and have explored this so-called point of dialogue by showing how Jordan and I confronted each other and learned to understand each other while recognizing our differences too. Throughout this book, the reader should be able to observe the encounter, the push and pull of the relationship, and to understand the process of how we came to understand and recognize each other. As narrator, I have paid careful attention to the translation of experience into words, and I have used anecdotes and dialogue to create this translation. And, as an anthropologist who instructs undergraduates, I have chosen to tell of events that I shared with Jordan that teach about life in modern Malawi. The dialogues are essential to display Jordan's wonderful character and to unravel the encounter. Jordan's voice and personality come through in all of them, I believe.

Some readers may experience this book as a memoir. But memoirs usually are self-indulgent and applaud their writers, and in this narrative neither Jordan nor I emerges as a hero. Some may see the book as a life history. In fact it covers only two short periods in two lives and is quite incomplete as a biography.

For me, when I step back from the exploration of the encounter, *Bambo Jordan* simply becomes a book that examines friendship across status and culture and (I hope) is a good story. As an anthropologist who teaches in the most humanistic of the disciplines of the social sciences, I hope that Jordan's story results in a greater understanding of all people who struggle so hard to survive.

The names used in *Bambo Jordan* are the real names of the individuals involved with the exception of Dan and Dr. Johnson who are portrayed somewhat negatively. Anthropologists are committed to protecting their informants; and even though I was not acting as an anthropologist when I was absorbing the information in this book, I have tried to make sure that none of the events selected will cause any major embarrassment. While this selection calls for judgment and is a risk, the reader can be assured that the events happened and have been truthfully related. Jordan himself is aware that I have written this book about him and has asked on several occasions when he will receive his copy. I am confident he will be pleased with this generally positive portrayal and ignore with equanimity and complete self-assurance those few instances which show him less favorably.

Reprinted by permission of The Dushkin Publishing Group, Inc. from Dr. F. Jeffress Ramsay, Editor, *Africa, Fifth Edition* from the Annual Editions Global Studies Series, Copyright © 1993 by The Dushkin Publishing Group, Inc., Guilford, Connecticut.

Chapter One

Getting Found

Beneath the mango and blue gum trees some thirty yards away from our quarters, dozens of men were lounging, seemingly unaffected by September's intense heat. At breakfast, when their presence had first registered with us, there had been fewer than ten; but now, as the sun was scorching the barren clay ground that separated us, the group had grown fivefold. They pushed themselves back under the leathery green leaves of the small mango trees to avoid the direct sun and chatted and occasionally laughed among themselves, but their eyes never strayed from us as we went about our business. We knew why they were there.

Our quarters were simple, with twenty-four rusty metal beds, mattresses dirty and sagging, a few wooden chairs scattered about six rooms, and a dining room so small we were forced to eat in shifts. But each room had a working lightbulb, and there was a toilet, and a bathtub offering hot water—as long as someone remembered to fire up the wood-burning stove. As promised, insects were everywhere, especially at night, but so too were the little lizards that came from the rafters to swallow them whole. The food was edible, *nsima* [a thick corn porridge] and cold toast—Africa and Britain joined on the dinner table, and though the conditions were spartan, we put up with them, knowing we would soon be moving on. On the covered veranda, or *khonde*, where we seemed to gather between walks to town to buy up nearly everything the shops had to offer, we could cool ourselves from the unrelenting heat and compare our purchases—lanterns, tin plates, blankets—all the items we hoped would insure our survival in the years ahead. Bernie darted about, anxiously checking and rechecking the supplies

7

stored in our most prized possession, a huge galvanized tub we would use to wash off the sweat of our labors.

As the day of our departure approached, all of us had grown increasingly nervous, a condition we tried to hide. I joked about sleeping from sundown to sunrise, for what else would one do at night? Others speculated about how they would read a book or even two each day to pass the time. And the questions proliferated: about food, snakes, accidents, malaria, jobs, communication, success, failure. We were ready to give it our best try, but the outcome would wait. Now the eve of our departure had arrived, and our excitement was evident as we made final preparations. Repacking suitcases and trunks, we rushed about, glancing to see what others had purchased to enhance their comfort. Constant small talk filled the air around our only map as we rechecked where friends had been posted and speculated about the virtues of our new homes—too hot, too isolated, too close to town.

Now and then I glanced up from my packing to where the crowd of men, of all ages, continued to circulate slowly beneath the trees. Their clothing was simple and well used, but it was thoughtfully chosen. They wore long-sleeved shirts and trousers, the costumes for gaining employment, and the sun treated them harshly for this. A bone-thin dog with a large gash over one ear came from the trees and walked onto the hot, open ground, but it stopped and turned back to the shade. I could see several men point and joke about its wise decision. This group had begun showing up at our little quarters days before, and as word of our arrival and the possibility of jobs began to circulate in town, their numbers grew, so that on this day there were some fifty men, all of them hoping for employment as cooks, houseboys, and gardeners. Now and then one would venture forward with letters of recommendation from a past employer, the lady of the household usually, outstretched before him. As soon as any of us stepped off the khonde to go into town, we would be met with a desperate plea for work, and as word spread that we would be departing the next day, the boldness increased. In time all of us were to be engaged in an exchange for which I, at least, was not prepared.

"Look at all those poor bastards, Bernie. They look sad. Just look at them, will you?"

"It's sad, all right. God, over the past few days there must have been two hundred of them here. And I don't think any one of them has been hired. Think we should hire one of them?"

"No. Let's stick to our plan to get some guy in Ntcheu. The people will surely get mad if we bring in an outsider."

Bernie simply nodded and kept playing with his battery-powered tape recorder. He looked up and restarted the conversation we had

had five or six times already: "Do you really think we should get a cook? Seriously?"

"Hell, I don't know. I'm confused. It is a bit much when you think about it." I added a new twist. "Say, Bernie, did you ever have a real job? I mean, after you got out of graduate school? I mean did you ever hire anybody for a job?"

He chuckled. He had done neither, and while no serious reply was necessary, he spoke. "Thinking about having a cook when you make only $112 a month is really crazy. It doesn't make any sense. But then these guys must really need jobs. And with the independence business, hundreds of British families are probably going to leave."

The issue was complicated, and most troubling was the idea of even having a cook or personal servant. Again he went back over familiar ground, "You sort of think servants are only for expatriates and rich Malawians. Certainly not for guys like us at the bottom of the heap. It's too bossy. Who are we to tell some guy to wash our underwear?"

"I agree, Bernie. Then again, what about all those other arguments? They save you a lot of time. Cooking on a wood stove is tough, especially when you've got to cut up the wood, and going to the market about every day is a pain, and they are watchmen for your house when you are not there."

Bernie had heard it all before. He simply continued packing his tape recorder while he nodded to indicate his familiarity with the arguments.

"Hey, do you know what a *mphutsi* fly is?" I went on.

"No, what's that?"

"It's a fly that lays its larvae in your clothes after you've washed them. It can happen on sheets, too. Things like that. When you wear those clothes, the larva bores into your skin and lives in there until it hatches out and flies away. Nice bugs, huh?"

"Where did you hear that?"

"Al and the guys were talking about it yesterday. Sounds horrible to me."

"So what are you supposed to do about it?"

"You've got to iron everything—absolutely everything. So what I'm saying is, a cook would be really useful for ironing." I paused for a few seconds to let Bernie fully comprehend my thoughts. Hire a cook to get the ironing done. "You know another thing I heard? I heard that all these cooks and houseboys sort of have servants too. When they are working in towns, they hire other guys in the villages to do the gardening and hoeing for them. I mean, it seems like nearly everyone has a servant. At least it's sort of that way."

My revelations completed, I sat down beside Bernie.

"Hey, Bernie, one of the guys here wants to talk to you and Bruce." I looked up from where I was sitting and glanced at Bernie, both of us obviously confused by the call. Who could possibly want us? Having just arrived, we knew no one. He returned my glance, and then we stood and walked along the khonde to meet one of the houseboys employed to help serve food and clean up after us. He bowed his head ever so slightly. His hands were gently clasped in front of his chest, and his shoulders rolled forward to complete the gesture. "*Zikomo* [Hello; Goodbye; Excuse me; Thank you; A friendly thought to you], bwana. Zikomo, bwana," each of us was greeted in turn.

"Zikomo, bambo," the reply from each of us, following the ritual of polite greetings so important in Malawi.

"*Muli bwanji* [How are you], bwana?" the man asked.

"*Tili bwino* [We are well]." Now it was our turn. "Muli bwanji, bambo?"

"Tili bwino, bwana." Done. Now we could talk, and the man continued. "Bwana, cook want talk bwana William and bwana Saller to back." He gestured for us to follow him, which we did, amused with the slaughter of Bernie's name, Sarrel, by his interchange of the *l*'s and *r*'s.

As we stepped from the kitchen into the sun, a small, muscular man, clean and neat with trousers pressed, shirt unwrinkled, tie straight and correctly made, and even shoes hinting of a shine, stepped forward from among the men seated under the trees. He walked straight to us, confidently, while we, unaware of how he knew us, simply stood and awaited him.

"Hello, sirs. I am Jordan." His voice was clear, his smile big and infectious; he made us smile too. His eyes were quick and friendly, and he looked directly at us, not at the ground as did most of the other men.

"Muli bwanji, bambo Jordan," I said, starting through the round of greetings.

"I am well, sir," He replied in English. "It is very wonderful, indeed, that you can speak Chichewa. How did you come to learn the Chichewa language so well?"

"We studied it at a university in the United States for three months. We don't speak much," Bernie replied.

"All we can say is 'Muli bwanji,' " I blurted out, with a slight laugh covering up more of the truth than I cared to admit.

"I did not know that people speak Chichewa in the United States," Jordan continued, his eyes widening to indicate his astonishment and his frown also exaggerated, signaling that he knew full well the situation.

"Students from Malawi who are at university in the States taught us a little, but we're really just beginners," Bernie added.

"Well, sirs, I can teach you Chichewa. I speak English very good, and I can know too many languages."

"What languages can you speak, Jordan?" I asked.

"I can speak Chichewa, Nyanja, Yao, Timbuka and Ngoni. I am Ngoni by tribe, so I am knowing this language. But only the old people speak this language to this day. I am speaking two Rhodesia languages—Shona and Ndebele."

"Well, Jordan, we only speak one language. I guess we're not too smart. How did you learn these languages?" I continued.

"Well, sir, I have a quick tongue to the languages. It is easy to me."

"Did you learn them in school?" I asked, beginning to enjoy our conversation.

"Well, no, sir. I learned them a little bit, a little bit when I was a cook boy to Rhodesia, and so I just learned them."

"When were you in Rhodesia?" Bernie asked.

"First time, 1951. Then 1953 to 1955."

"What did you do there?" Bernie continued.

"I was just a garden boy in 1951. But in 1953 I was the garden boy, and Mrs. Morrison could see how neat and clever I was. She made me to be a houseboy. Then she sacked the cook, and I am the cook for the two years."

"Did she teach you to be a cook?" I asked.

"Yes, sir. Well, actually, I can cook just a bit already before I go to Rhodesia."

"How did you learn to cook a little bit?" I continued.

"Mrs. Smith at Gowa Mission taught me. Do you know this place, Gowa Mission?"

"No, we don't know Gowa Mission. Where's Gowa Mission?"

"It is to Ntcheu, sirs, near to my village. I went there to school, old standard three only. So the Reverend Smith and Mrs. Smith know me. They give me job as a houseboy because I was, well, I was such a clever chap. I am clean, too, as you can see. Mrs. Smith then she teached me, I should say taught me, cooking. A little this, a little that, but not too much. So I learned to be a cook. It is easy for me."

"Why aren't you still there? When was this?" I asked two questions this time.

He paused to think. "It was to nineteen hundred and forty eight, I believe, sir."

"Why did you leave?" I repeated my question.

"This is just a little bit complicated." He put me off a bit but continued. "You know these missionary people. They can be very nice people, but . . ." his voice trailed off in mid-sentence.

"But what?" my inquiry continued.

"Well, sir, I take them to be very nice people, but these missionary people cannot be nice to us Africans. I should say not all missionaries. Mrs. Smith was a too good lady, I know, but she can be very set in the way she is doing. It was no good job. Really, sir. She always wanted us Africans to do this, do that. Ah, I did not like."

"Did she let you drink?" I said in jest.

"Oh, no, sir." Jordan's face was tense, no hint he understood my comment to be playful.

"Do you drink?"

"Well, yes sir. A little bit."

"Never trust a man who doesn't drink, Jordan. Did you ever hear that?"

"Well, no, sir. I did not." He was confused.

"Just a crazy expression. Never mind."

"OK, sir." He seemed relieved that no reply was needed.

"What can we do for you, Jordan?" Bernie turned to business.

"Well, sirs, I wish to be your cook. I am a too good cook boy."

We knew this was coming, and while I guessed Bernie was enjoying Jordan as much as I was, we had no time to discuss it between ourselves. I asked, to stall things a bit, "How did you know our names?"

"Well, sir, I am coming to here yesterday, and I can see many cook boys, and that it is difficult for me. Today I go to the office of Peaci Corpsi and have meeting with the big bwana. When I talked to him, I asked if bwanas were going to Ntcheu and for the names. This is how I know the name."

"Pretty damn smart, bambo. But I don't think we really know what we're going to do," I said. "You see, we want to hire someone from Ntcheu when we get there."

"But I am from Ntcheu. For my whole life I live to Ntcheu. We Ngoni people live there to this place. I can know all the people, and I am the best cook to Ntcheu."

"I thought your village was close to Gowa Mission. Is Gowa Mission near the *boma* [rural government center]?" I asked.

"Well, yes, sir. It is just there on the lower side."

"How far is your village from the boma?"

"Approximately ten miles, I can say, sir."

"That seems far away to me, Jordan. How do you get from your village to the boma?"

"By footing, sir."

"Don't you have a bicycle?" I continued my questions.

"No, sir. For my whole life I have no bicycle."

"So you don't know the people at the boma, then?"

"Oh yes, sir. I know all the people to Ntcheu. I am a very good cook, sir, and the people can know me to be so." He was pressing, understandably.

"Well, maybe we can talk it over," Bernie said slowly, glancing over to me. I nodded in agreement but remained skeptical about departing from our original plan.

"Sirs, I have the letters of reference and many papers for working for you to see."

He reached quickly and carefully into his shirt pocket and pulled out a small stack of papers that had been carefully folded and I assume carefully guarded over the years. He handed them to Bernie who had remained serious throughout our little talk and who Jordan probably guessed was the one to convince.

"Well, bambo, we're going to go back to our room to discuss this for a few minutes," I said, hoping that Bernie was in agreement and sensing that our conversation had gone far enough to warrant a private talk. "You wait here, OK?"

"Yes, bwana. I can wait, sir."

Jordan turned and walked slowly back to the trees where he had been standing. The eyes of the many men followed him closely. We turned and walked back through the kitchen to the khonde.

"What do you think, Bernie?" I asked as I sat down on the khonde's edge. "Seems like a good guy to me."

"These letters are real good," Bernie mumbled as he lowered himself to sit beside me. "Of course, all the expatriates probably write great letters," he added after a little more reading.

"Yeah, probably," I said. "Then again all these fine British ladies who sit on their asses all day probably took this cook business very seriously. You know what I mean? What else did they have to do all day except keep three or four servants in motion? Probably still have some weird ideas about proper British culture and their civilizing mission."

"Probably true." Bernie nodded and mumbled again as he continued to read through the last of the letters, obviously more concerned with the references than with my speculations.

I read the papers next and then turned to Bernie, who had been waiting for me to finish. "Well, what do you want to do?" Bernie asked.

"Hell, let's hire the guy. He's from Ntcheu. And he speaks very well. And he's neat. He's got to be a lot smarter than the rest of these guys. I mean he's a hustler." I waited a moment and then provided the final rationalization. "Besides, we're probably not going to do any better when we get there. And God, there's something about him that's nice, and I guess I just like him."

"I agree," Bernie said. "He's nice and seems smart. And I liked him too. Let's do it."

We stood and walked back out through the kitchen. Jordan immediately came forward, looking straight into each of our faces to get a clue as to our decision. Without saying a word, I passed him his papers.

An awkward moment passed, Bernie and I not knowing who would speak. "OK, Jordan, we'd like to hire you as our cook," I finally said.

"Oh, jolly good, bwana." Jordan's smile was big and beautiful. "I can be a very good cook to you. Yes, bwana, I will do a too good job. Do my bosses wish me to help now?"

"No, I think we're OK for now, Jordan, but I think we need to talk about your salary," Bernie said, seriously. "How much do you want?"

"Whatever you think is correct, sir."

"Well," I mumbled softly, indicating my confusion. "Well, I don't know what's fair. What do cooks make these days? I mean, we want to be fair." Jordan did not speak but the intensity of his look let us know that the issue of salary was taken every bit as seriously as the hiring itself.

"We've never hired anyone before to be a cook, Jordan. What do you think is fair?" Bernie repeated our opening position.

Jordan came back, "Well, sirs, that is not for me to say. You are the bosses. I must listen to you."

Back to us again. I knew we had to start someplace so I spoke. "Well, Jordan, the cooks who are working here now have been asking for jobs too. They seem to be asking for four pounds per month. At least this is what I seem to be hearing."

He looked at me but gave no indication of his feelings. After a quick glance at Bernie I said, "What do you think? Is this OK, four pounds per month?"

"Well, sir, it is a little bit all right." He paused to organize his thoughts. Extremely important negotiations like this required skill. He knew he had little bargaining power with so many men standing about willing to accept such a job. But he probably knew we were inexperienced in such matters and that his real chance was to appeal to our sense of fair play.

He continued softly, politely, but without hesitation. "You see, sir, these boys here are not real cook boys. No. They just do simple cooking and cleaning. Can they make cakes and pastries? No, sir, they can't. Can they bake bread? Can they read the recipes and cook for American bwanas? No, they cannot."

We looked at each other and he went on. "You see, sirs, I am a real cook." His emphasis on *real* was not lost on me as he continued to talk and persuade. "I keep the house very clean and do all the washing and ironing in just one day." He let us reflect on this and continued, "Can these boys do the marketing? No, I do not think. You see, sir, there is no madam, so I can do all the marketing, and I Jordan can do all the meals just the way you like. I can know too many recipes."

He stopped and waited for us to speak, but we simply stood looking, beginning to be captivated, but not knowing what one was supposed to say.

He went on. "And I am a very honest chap, my bwanas. Since all my years as cook boy not one penny is missing. And I do not eat the bwanas' food. Sure. It is true. I am a very honest fellow."

"OK, OK, we believe you. You are a very good cook, we can see that," I said to slow him down. To lighten things a bit I added, "But, Jordan, can you cook a pizza?"

His forehead wrinkled and his voice changed slightly. "What is this pizza? I do not know such a thing."

"It's an Italian thing we eat in the United States. It's sort of bread with tomato sauce and has cheese on it. It's baked in the oven." Bernie offered in brief explanation.

"Well, sir, I do not know this thing, but I am sure I can make. I can learn too quickly these things."

"Good, I bet you can, Jordan, but still we want to pay you fairly. We know you're a good cook, so what do you think is fair?" I brought the conversation back to the matter at hand.

"Well, I must let my bosses say," he replied, refusing to indicate an amount but surely knowing that he was going to get more.

"How does six pounds sound?" Bernie spoke up.

"That can be a little bit all right, sir," He looked at Bernie with the same expression as before, the one that seemed to say that the discussion was not over as far as he was concerned.

"Goddammit, Jordan, how much do you want? Just say, for God's sake." I jumped in, trying to conclude this craziness over a few dollars.

"Well . . . ," he paused, but then went on. "Well, I can like a bit more, sirs."

"How much more? Fifty pounds? Tell us what you have in mind." I spoke sharply, not realizing that we were the ones beginning to do the begging. My annoyance was not over the small sums we were discussing and he, who saw us as so rich, probably knew this. I simply wanted to come to a fair agreement and to be done with it, and he probably realized this too.

"What do you want, Jordan? Come on, just say, will you?" I continued to press.

"What do you say to seven pounds per month?" Bernie spoke up. "Let's make it seven pounds per month to begin with. If you do a good job, we will give you a raise soon. Is this OK? Seven pounds per month?''

"Well, that can be OK, sir, if you say. Well, what can I say, sir? If you give seven pounds to me, it is seven pounds. It is a little bit all right.''

"Good, Jordan. It's a deal.'' I reached out my hand, we shook hands, and he smiled. Bernie did the same, and the smile continued.

"So now what?'' I asked. "You see, we'll be leaving for Ntcheu tomorrow by truck. How can you get to Ntcheu, Jordan?''

"Well, sir, I can take the night compost and meet you in Ntcheu when we arrive.''

"What's the night compost?'' Bernie and I asked in unison.

"It is the compost. The night bus, sirs. It leaves I should say about seven o'clock. It arrives to Ntcheu about half one in the night. So Ida and I can go by bus and meet you tomorrow.''

"Who's Ida?'' I asked quickly.

"She is my wife, sir. She and the three little children are with me here. They will return to Ntcheu with Ida and me.''

"How many kids do you have, Jordan?'' I asked, not having thought that he might be married and have children.

"I have six children, sir.''

"Six kids. Where are the rest of them?''

"In the village, sir. They are at my village. That is, I should say they are at my home, which is the village of Ida. It is the sister to Ida who can be watching them.''

"Boy, six kids. How old are you anyway?''

"Well, sir.'' He thought for a few moments. "I should be maybe thirty-three or thirty-five, sir. Yes, it can be thirty-three.''

"So you and Ida and the three kids can take the bus, and we will meet you there tomorrow.'' Bernie reviewed it all for us.

"Yes, sir, I can do this. We will meet tomorrow in Ntcheu at the boma.''

"OK, then, we will see you all tomorrow.'' Bernie went on, trying to conclude things, "I don't know where we'll be, but I think we will be at the rest house for a few days. Do you know where the rest house is in Ntcheu, Jordan?''

"Yes, sir. I do.''

"Good, we'll see you there.''

"OK, sir,'' he replied seriously. Then he added softly. "But, sir, I have no money for bus. You see, I have not been working for these many months, and so I can have no money.''

Bernie and I looked at each other. Finally Bernie asked, "Well, how much do you need for the bus fares, for all five of you?''

"I do not know, sir,'' he replied thoughtfully.

"Well, I guess we can give you some money,'' Bernie said, looking to me to get my approval.

"How much are you going to need for the bus?" I asked.

"It can be very expensive, sir. And I would like to do a little shopping while I am here. You see things are very dear to Ntcheu."

"OK, OK, but how much do you need?" Were we back to this again? I wondered.

"How's ten pounds sound, for the whole business?" Bernie interjected.

"That can be very fine, sir," Jordan replied quickly. "Ten pounds will be all right."

I knew Bernie's offer was most generous, but it did not seem to matter.

"Here, Jordan, take the ten pounds." Bernie's voice was nearly as quick as his hand, which was already passing over the bills.

"Oh, thank you, sir. Thank you, very much. This should be sufficient." He counted the money very carefully and shoved it deep inside the front pockets of his trousers and looked back to each of us.

"So we're all set then, Jordan? We will meet you tomorrow in Ntcheu," I said to conclude things.

"Yes, bwana, I will meet you tomorrow. But there is one more matter I wish to speak to you about." He kept things going.

"What's that?" I said, confused.

"Well, sir. It is the matter of my *phoso*."

"Your what?"

"My phoso, sir."

"What's a phoso?"

"It is the money you pay me each week so that I may buy my food."

We looked at each other.

"What do you mean money to buy your food? I thought your monthly salary was to buy your food?"

"Well, sir, it is just a little bit like that. But we boys also receive phoso each week for food and soap and things such as that."

"You mean we pay you a salary each month, and then we pay you each week too?" The pitch of my voice was raised.

"Ah, huh," Jordan replied quickly, "it is like that."

"What kind of a crazy system is this? Why don't you just get more each month?" I spoke quickly—a legitimate question, I reasoned.

"Well, sir, this is the way the people do it. I should say these European madams who are bossing the households pay their boys like this," Jordan explained.

"But why?" I remained confused.

"Well, I think in the old days, I should say today too, sir, the boys can spend all their money just like that, drinking and buying the goods such as cloth and whatnot. Just a little bit of food too. It is the madams' way that boys will have enough money for food all the month. Some of these chaps they just cannot manage the money.''

"But you can manage. Right? Unlike the other guys." I came back quickly, realizing that this system would obviously encourage its own use, the domestics quickly learning to depend on it and so demonstrating to the colonialists that Africans were into quick gratification and lacked the ability to handle money.

"Yes. I can manage the money. This is true. But this is how it is to Malawi."

Bernie looked at me. His eyebrows went up over his glasses and stayed up. He turned to Jordan. "Well, how much is this phoso thing? What do cooks get each week for their extra payment?"

"Well, sir. Whatever. I cannot just say." Jordan's reply was as consistent and steady as ever. Once again we were going to make offers, and he would negotiate cleverly to the end.

"Come on, Jordan." I found myself aggressive, but I was pleading. "Tell us what you want. No bullshit, OK? Just tell us what's fair."

"I believe that five shillings a week would be fair." He spoke softly, but directly, his eyes never leaving mine.

"Sounds fair to me," I came right back. "What do you think, Bern?"

"Great. Sounds good to me too." His reply was as quick as mine. I guessed he had given up, like me.

Jordan seemed relieved. He did not smile, but a little tension seemed to go from his face.

"So that's it. Seven pounds per month and five shillings a week. Right, Jordan?" Bernie summed it all up once again.

"That is correct, sir."

"So we'll see you tomorrow in Ntcheu then. OK, Jordan?" I said.

"OK, sir. I can see my bwanas tomorrow at the rest house to Ntcheu."

Finished at last, we smiled at each other and all shook hands, even Bernie and I for fun.

"Go well," we wished Jordan in Chichewa.

"Remain well," he replied. The handshakes and the proper expressions for parting completed, we turned slowly to return to the shade of the khonde.

"One thing, sir," Jordan's voice softer than ever. "If I may say, sirs."

"What, Jordan?" I answered, a hint of fear in my voice.

He hesitated. "It is this, sir. You see I had no money for these many months. And the kids they seem to need some clothes so as not to be little pickaninnies. And my Ida she needs some cloth for the dresses so she can be as smart as I am for the new bosses. Well, the materials to Ntcheu are very dear, sir, as I said to you. I know this to be true. I was wishing my good bosses could borrow me two pounds so I can shop here to Blantyre, where I take the things to be cheaper."

A big pause. Bernie and I stared at Jordan, then at each other. "Pickaninnies." My surprise at this strange word was so great that I started to laugh as I said it. "God, we don't want your kids to be pickaninnies. Damn, that would be tricky to be one of those. Don't you think, Bern?"

"Yeah, that would be bad." Bernie could barely speak, but Jordan's face remained as serious as ever.

"Why not, I guess. I mean, what's the difference. We'll just give you five pounds at the end of the month, then." It seemed reasonable to me. Things probably were cheaper here, and he probably needed these things as he said. So without asking Bernie, I reached into my pocket and took out two pounds and handed them over. Jordan took them in his hands, gently. This was no wild grab for money. Just an exchange for services which would come later.

"So that's it then, Jordan. There's nothing else is there? I mean you don't need a new suit or anything, do you?" The sarcasm was inappropriate, and I regretted it immediately.

But it was the opening Jordan needed. "Well, sir, I believe I will need a new apron for my duties."

"An apron?" My eyes widened as I spoke.

"Yes, sir. You see, sir, we cook boys need an apron for the duties. For the cooking and like that. So the clothes can remain clean and to dress smart like a cook."

"How much is an apron?" It was Bernie's turn now.

"I should say, four or five shillings, sir. I may have the khonde tailors here in the town make me one before I take the night *basi* [bus]. It can be very cheap here. But not to Ntcheu."

"What are khonde tailors?" Bernie asked.

"You have seen the tailors, I am sure, boss. They are the boys who sit to front of the shops to town and do the sewing," he explained.

"What do you do?" Bernie continued.

"I can go to the shop and buy the good material. Then one of these tailors will just make me the apron. I will instruct him. It is very simple. Sure."

"Why not, I guess." Bernie groaned for obvious effect and then pulled out the five shillings in coin, counting it slowly as he handed it over. His unfamiliarity with the new money was as obvious as his willingness to pass it along, it seemed. Then, with his fingers outstretched and the last of the coins resting openly in his palm, he asked, "What else do you need, Jordan? This is it. You might as well get the rest of them." He burst into laughter and I joined in immediately. It was a good laugh.

Jordan smiled, maybe even laughed with us a little, but when we regained our control, he spoke with the same seriousness as always. "Well, Bwana, there is the matter of the phoso this week. I mean I must buy my food and soap for this week as you, my bosses, know."

"Of course you do, Jordan," I said, still laughing, but in more control than Bernie. "Bernie, give him another five shillings for his phoso." Bernie's arm went out slowly to Jordan, his palm open.

"Just take what you need," Bernie said, "we'll settle up in a couple of years or something." Again the laughter began from Bernie. Up and down went his shoulders, and his face reddened, and his eyes shut as he laughed over every inch of himself. Again I joined him, and then most of the cooks standing under the trees did the same. Only Jordan's face remained serious. This was a critical and sensitive undertaking because his initial pay would have a bearing on all his subsequent earnings, and he knew this. More important was his getting what he wanted without our feeling exploited. To work as someone's cook was a very intimate relationship, since the cook would live right at the home of the boss seven days a week. To make it tolerable, enjoyable if possible, the servant must use all his intelligence and guile to create a favorable situation. It would be a long and delicate process, shaped a little each day by the servant. In this first encounter, Jordan had his money and had us laughing too. It was a good beginning for him.

"So, bambo Jordan. You've got all our shekels. Are you happy? I mean, is there anything else before we go inside?" Bernie's face was still red as he tried to end it once and for all.

"What are these shekels, sir?"

"Skip it, Jordan," Bernie said to end it.

"OK, sir."

"Anything else, bambo?" I asked.

"No, sir. There's nothing else."

"So we'll see you tomorrow in Ntcheu. Right?"

"Right, sir. I will be going then. Bye. Bye. Sirs."

"Bye, Jordan." We both spoke.

We stood and watched him turn and walk away toward the trees. One of the men sitting there rose to talk to him. Probably someone he had just met.

"Let's get out of here." I tapped Bernie on the arm, and we walked quickly away.

On the khonde again, we stood and looked at each other for a moment. Bernie shook his head and chuckled. "We did it. A good guy, I guess."

"I agree. It's pretty funny, though. I mean when you think about it, he's doubled his salary, and he hasn't started to work."

"And he's got ten goddamn pounds of ours, too."

"Twelve, really," I said.

"Actually, he's got twelve pounds five. Hell, we're giving him more just to get to work than we're going to give him for a month's work. Crazy, really crazy." He burst out laughing, and I joined in with him again.

It was done. The hiring was over. We had committed ourselves for the time being to this little cook from Ntcheu. For me it was to last for another thirty years, and maybe longer. It was to make my life fuller, simply better. Jordan's too, I think.

Chapter Two

The End of the Earth

The lorry began to shake violently, and Bernie and I reached out to steady ourselves and our trunks. We were slowing down, and the lorry was no longer capable of riding along the crests of the corrugations in the dirt road. The wheels plunged down into each trough, slamming into the backside of the next rise, and each part of the lorry seemed to jump independently of the others. As we slowed more, the lorry settled into a less random set of movements, and the driver, in full control again, glanced back through the cab's window to make sure we were still aboard.

We turned left down a little hill onto an even narrower and rougher dirt road. This was the entrance to the boma itself, and the sights of a simple little community both appalled and delighted me. The road was lined with majestic jacaranda trees, and their lilac blue blossoms filled each tree beautifully while their orderly placement showed the planning of some forgotten administrator from decades before. The new Malawian district commissioner probably saw no need to keep the boma like an English garden, when there were so many other projects to do, and the flowering orange bougainvillea and brilliant red flame trees and bamboo trees were now overgrown and seemed to close in around us.

Scattered about were little red brick houses with roofs of dull green corrugated iron, mixed with a few shiny roofs from which the sun shot off like mirrors. The houses were situated strangely, as if there was no plan. On the left, two double rows lined each side of a football field and the houses were neat and well kept and appeared large enough to contain several rooms. But further along the roadway, older, smaller, and shabbier houses whose brick had turned dark were scattered throughout. They were placed closely together, and we could see women working and children playing in the tiny courtyards behind the buildings. Fires burned under blackened aluminum pots, and children ran and played with homemade wire toys or old tennis balls while the adult women cooked or pounded maize or sewed clothing as they watched their young children. There were large government buildings, a hospital, a secondary and a primary school, a small prison, a district commissioner's office, and a public works building. But most interesting were the people—families, children coming from school, travelers on bicycles, men in strange uniforms, men sitting under trees playing games with stones, women carrying large clay pots filled with water—people active and vibrant, a real community.

The truck stopped before an old brick building with a long, prominent, covered khonde. This was the office of the district commissioner, and as the center of the district's government it was a busy place. Men in uniforms sat on benches outside the main office and were an impressive sight with heavy black boots; khaki kneesocks, shorts, and shirts; broad leather belts; and each with an impressive red fez, tassel and all. They were messengers, I later learned, and they rode bicycles throughout the district, sometimes up to forty miles in a single direction to bring official information from the district office to a village headman or even to a villager.

We stood, perplexed, for a few moments, but relief came quickly when a chubby young man in his mid-twenties, dressed in a well-pressed black suit that could not reach around his waist, bounced down the stairs of the boma and came toward us with the confidence of a man in charge.

"Hello, I am Jere, district officer of Ntcheu. I am here to greet you to our little place here." His hand went out to each of us, and we began all the hand shaking and greetings required of us all.

He confirmed that Bernie and I would be staying in the local rest house for a few days until our house was ready and hoped our stay in Ntcheu would be a pleasant one. We chattered briefly about our journey and the weather and the beauty of Malawi and how it compared with the United States. We were polite to one another, but it soon became clear that nothing of substance would transpire. Mr. Jere turned from us, and commands were shouted out in the direction of the khonde where five men, shoeless but dressed in khaki shirts and shorts, stepped forward quickly and stood rigidly at attention. The orders continued, rapidly in Chichewa. "Take the bwanas' *katundu* [luggage] to the rest house. Be careful. Do it quickly. Make sure it is safe."

"*Inde* [Yes], bwana," they replied in soft voices, eyes cast downward. We pointed to our luggage, and they grabbed it quickly and hoisted it up on their heads. The suitcases, boxes, and tub were gone in a moment. We watched them move quickly away while Mr. Jere instructed us to follow them. We made our farewells to the lorry driver and Mr. Jere and set off for our temporary home.

We walked along the deeply rutted dirt road lined with tall cedars and colorful bushes, until we came to a small white sign that identified the rest house. It was a plain, red brick building some thirty feet on each side with a gray iron roof. To the right was a smaller building and the smoke that poured from both the chimney and its only door indicated it was the kitchen. The space around the rest house was without grass and the ground was hard and well worn.

We approached timidly, not knowing where we were to go. To our great relief, Jordan appeared in the doorway with a big smile and a warm welcome.

As the three of us walked inside the rest house, we entered a large square room with whitewashed walls and no pictures. It had four big, plain wooden chairs, with arm rests, placed around a small coffee table. Beyond this sitting room was a dining room with a large wooden table and seven sturdy upright chairs. To one side there was a kerosene refrigerator and a sideboard containing dishes and silverware. The back wall had two large casement windows, and to the left and right were doors. Jordan directed us to the one on the right.

Upon entering, we discovered that our luggage had been neatly placed in the center of the room. Along the sides were four iron beds, over which mosquito nets were tied in a simple knot and suspended from the rafters of the high ceiling. At night these nets would be lowered and tucked in around the mattresses to keep us protected from insects, which were abundant most of the year. Jordan pointed out that the room was quite luxurious because it contained a small bathroom with a sink and tub, as well as a separate water closet.

Bernie and I quickly moved our boxes and trunks against the walls and placed our suitcases onto the two beds we decided not to use for sleeping. With that completed, Jordan spoke. "You know, my bosses, there can be no food here for you my bwanas to eat." After a pause to let us understand, he continued. "The people buy the food to the shops and the cook here is cooking for the bwanas. This can be the way of this place, sirs. We can go to Mphate to the Indian shops to buy the food." He stopped and waited for us to reply.

"Well how far is this Mphate place, Jordan?" I asked.

"It is just there, bwana. Along the Blantyre-Lilongwe Road," he replied.

"But how far is it?" I asked.

"I should say it can be a mile, sir. It is a little bit like that. About a mile or two miles, I should say.''

I tried a new approach. ''How long does it take to walk to the market, then?''

''Oh, it is but a jolly short walk.'' He informed me.

''How long does a jolly short walk take?'' I inquired.

''Oh, I should say it can be ten minutes or five minutes. Yes, it should be that.''

''Well, Jordan, if you go outside, can you see Mphate from here?''

''Well, yes, you can, sir. I should say if you walk to the main road, sir, you can see to the shops. It can be just there, a little bit.''

''Well, Jordan, I really don't feel like going right now,'' I replied, and Bernie nodded his head in agreement. ''We'll give you some money, and you can walk up and get what you think we need. Does that sound OK?''

''Yes, it is a bit all right, sir. I, Jordan, can go and you my bwanas can remain for resting. It can be.''

I reached into my pocket and took out a five pound note and handed it to him. ''Do you think this will be enough?'' I asked.

''Yes, this can be sufficient, sir.'' He hesitated but asked, ''What do my bwanas like for the food?''

Bernie spoke quickly, ''I don't think it really matters, Jordan. Just get some food for tonight and for breakfast tomorrow. Then tomorrow we can all go and look around and get some more things.''

''Do my bosses like the tinned food? You see, these Indian shops can have tins, and I take it that the Europeans like this food. Is this so, boss?''

''I guess we like it, Jordan. But we like food from the market, too. So just buy some potatoes and meat and bread and some margarine in a tin. That will do for tonight. OK?'' Bernie answered.

''This is what I can do, boss.'' He hesitated and went on, ''But, sir, what kind of meat do my bwanas like?''

''No goat meat,'' I said quickly. ''Anything but goat meat. We like steak and chicken. If you can get these, get them. All right?''

''Sir, the steak. I do not know. How can I say. Well, the meat it is not the steak as my bwanas know.''

''But the Ngoni people are cattle people, aren't they? There must be steak here.''

Jordan seemed confused. ''Yes, we have this cattle meat as my bwana says. You see, boss, this meat is too tough indeed. No, you cannot eat. It can be too tough. We Africans can eat, but no, not you, my bwanas.''

''Just buy some cattle meat if it's not too tough. If not, then buy a chicken. If you can't get any meat, we will eat bread and use our peanut butter.''

Jordan indicated that he understood and he began to move

toward the door. "Zikomo, bwana. *Ndapita* [I am going]."

"But what about you, Jordan? Do you need some food?" Bernie inquired.

"Yes, boss, I can," he replied quickly.

"Well, get yourself something too. Say, where's Ida and the kids? Where are you staying?" Bernie continued.

"Ah, my Ida and the kids have returned to the village. I can stay just here. I know so many people to this place that I am with a man to my village who works to the Indian shops. My Ida she will come after the week when my bwanas have the place to stay." This explained, he bade us goodbye and departed.

I was relieved to be alone. While we had done very little this day, the move was stressful, and my fear of living in isolation in this little boma increased when I realized just how small the community was. We talked to each other very little for the next half hour. Bernie took out his tape recorder and aimlessly played with it while I simply sat on the edge of the bed and stared into space.

It was not long before Bernie and I had fallen asleep.

As I awoke from my sleep, I heard someone moving around in our room. Slowly, I became aware that it was Jordan. He had returned from Mphate and, with the enthusiasm of a new employee, he began the chores he thought necessary. Holding the dirty laundry, which I had thrown into a heap on the floor, in one hand and a box of soap powder in the other, he looked down at me as I struggled again to open my eyes.

"Hello, boss."

"Hi, Jordan. What's up? How was your shopping?" I began to sit up.

"It is OK. I have bought the things for my bwanas, and so I have returned." He continued, "I have purchased the potatoes and bananas and mangoes. And the bread and a tin of coffee and the milk powder and the three eggs. And I have the nsima for your Jordan." As he was about to leave, he turned and spoke, "Are the bosses OK?"

"What do you mean, bambo?" I asked.

Jordan hesitated but did not look at either of us. An awkward moment passed as we awaited his reply. "The bosses can be too tired, isn't it?"

"We just need to rest a little. It was a long trip, and we just need to be alone," I said.

"You can be tired from the trip?"

"I guess we're tired. Or maybe it's a little stress. Everything is so strange and new. It's a little confusing. A kind of culture shock,

I think. That's all." Bernie spoke this time.

"This place can be strange, my boss? I am not understanding."

"It's just that it's different. And, it's hard to know how to act. It's so small and far away from everything," Bernie continued.

"But there can be so many people to Ntcheu. So there is too much activity to this place."

I smiled. "I guess it's what you're used to. It just seems like the end of the earth to us, that's all."

Jordan's face became flushed. "The end of the earth, my boss?"

I replied quickly to cover myself. "I mean Ntcheu seems so far away and isolated that it's a little scary. I was just wondering how I'll live here for two years."

Jordan's face flushed even more. My comments had confused and hurt him, so I tried again. "What I mean, Jordan, is that we're sure there's lots happening here and that the people are very nice. It's just that we need to learn a little more. It's sort of frightening now, that's all."

"It is frightening, boss?"

"A little bit. Since we don't know anything or anybody," I continued.

"I am seeing just a little bit what the boss is speaking."

"Good. I'm sure you can. I mean, you must have felt confused when you first went to Rhodesia to work."

"Yes, I am seeing a bit, my boss."

Bernie joined in. "That's why we just want to be alone for a while. So don't worry about us."

Jordan's face returned to normal, and he nodded his head to indicate his understanding. He began to leave, but stopped again. "Your Jordan has worked too many jobs. It is difficult every time, this I can say. But the person can get used to and the newness can go. And so that place can be the home with the friends and the enjoyment. This I know to be so."

We both stared at him for a moment, and then I spoke. "Thanks, Jordan, very much. That's a nice thought. I hope you're right."

"I am knowing, my boss." He gently shut the door as he stepped from the room, and I felt a little better for his comments and his caring.

Chapter Three

Initiation Rites

"Damn, it's dark out here, Bernie."

"I'll say. I can't see the goddamn path. We'll never get back like this."

"Say, that was nice of Gene and Dan to have us over to dinner. Our first night in Ntcheu, and we get asked out. And that guy Bastone's a real trip. Why he lives with the headmaster and his wife and not in the house for the volunteers is strange, especially since they have three bedrooms. I'll bet he doesn't get along with Dan, since it's Dan who just came here." Bernie did not reply to my speculations. His concern with our walk seemed to be his only care.

I began to take very tiny steps and thrust my hands forward at about chest height as we went farther from the light of the house. "This is impossible," I said. "I really can't see a thing. Why the hell didn't we bring a flashlight?" I chattered on foolishly as we continued to shuffle along with great caution. "Should we go back and ask them to lend us a light?"

"I'd be too embarrassed. We'd look like greenhorns," Bernie said. "Most of the people walk around without lights. We ought to be able to do the same."

"Maybe so, but they know where they are going." My feeble reply did nothing to improve our situation, and soon we both stopped. I said, "We need a plan. We'll be all night getting to the rest house at this rate."

Bernie quickly developed a scheme. "Look. Let's stand beside each other and spread out until we each come to the edge, where we can feel the grass. Then we can move together a foot or two. If one of us gets off, the other can give a hint as to where the path

29

is. So keep talking.''

I agreed to try, and we spread out as planned and started again, taking little steps like blind men without canes, our hands again held forward to act as antennae. Our progress was slow until we reached the central dirt road that ran through the center of the boma. Here we discovered the ruts from the traffic, which gave us an important clue to our direction.

"You know, Bernie, what bothers me most?"

"What's that?"

"Snakes."

"Snakes?"

"Yeah, snakes. Someone told me a few days ago that snakes like to come out on the roads at night. Seems roads get warmed during the day and stay a little warmer than the grass along the side. So at night the snakes sometimes come out to stay warm. Unfortunately, that's where we are."

"Don't tell me that. That's all I need to hear." Bernie's voice was strained.

"Hey, that's what I heard. I'm not excited about this either, believe me," I said.

"What kind of snakes?"

"Who knows? All those big poisonous ones, I guess. Mambas and puff adders for all I know. Hey, I'm a city guy." He asked no more about it, and I guessed he, like me, was just being fatalistic.

The walk had scared me, and I was greatly relieved when we reached the rest house. It was an experience I was unprepared for, and I wondered if I would ever become adjusted to a life without lights.

We opened the door, and to our delight there was a small lantern on the dining room table, burning just above a flicker. The cook had done us a great service, and I realized again how unprepared we were for the darkness.

Suddenly we heard people laughing and as we walked into the dining area, we could see a bright light coming from beneath the door, which suddenly opened. A handsome, athletic-looking, well-dressed man stepped forward. "Hello. So you chaps are the new Peace Corps volunteers," he said.

"That's us," I said.

He extended his hand. "My name's Ian Mkandawire. I am the assistant district commissioner here in Ntcheu."

We shook hands and introduced ourselves.

"I saw you fellows this morning when you arrived. I guess you did not see me. How are you adjusting to our little place?"

We claimed we were doing fine, and we chatted comfortably for a few more minutes. It was delightful. This man was polished and extroverted and easy to talk to. Finally, he said there were two men we should meet, as they worked in Ntcheu too.

Ian stepped back into the room and spoke what I guessed was Tumbuka; at least I knew it was not Chichewa. Two men came forward with him into the dining area. Like Ian, they were in long-sleeved shirts and well-pressed slacks. "This is Oswald Ndovi. He works for the Ministry of Agriculture here. And this is Tony Chilemwe. He's an agricultural extension officer. Lives up the road about five miles."

This was a real surprise. These men were obviously well educated, and I was surprised that they were living in a rural area like Ntcheu and not in Blantyre.

"You chaps certainly have a lot of katundu here," Ian said as he nodded in the direction of our room.

"I guess so," Bernie answered as he opened our room's door wider. "We're just trying to be prepared."

"What is that thing?" Ian stepped forward and pointed to the battery-operated tape recorder.

"That's a tape recorder," Bernie answered again. "You know what that is?"

"No, I don't think so. A tape recorder?"

"Yes, you talk into it, and it plays back what you said," Bernie explained.

"I see." Ian spoke carefully as he continued to stare. "That seems to be a very complicated machine."

"Not really. Would you like to see how it works?" Bernie asked.

"That would be jolly nice."

Bernie moved quickly to insert four new batteries and to set the reel-to-reel tapes and to attach the microphone. Then buttons were pressed and Bernie began, "One, two, three, four, testing, testing." He rewound the reels and played it over.

Ian seemed amazed. "Oh, this is very good!" he said.

"It's just a tape recorder. You talk, and it plays back. You can record music even," Bernie continued to instruct.

"Well, this is quite a thing," Ian spoke with a touch of wonder.

"You try it, Ian," I said.

He hesitated, "No, I do not think so. I am not interested."

"No, go ahead, Ian. It's fun to hear yourself." I pressed him a little, and Bernie held the microphone close to Ian's face.

"Here. You just talk into this, and I'll play it back." Bernie joined me in urging Ian to try.

Ian hesitated again, but Bernie pressed the buttons and the reels began turning. "Go ahead. Just say something." Bernie was pleading.

Ian glanced around and then faced the question of what he might say.

"Go ahead. Just count to four," Bernie suggested.

Finally, he copied Bernie, "One, two, three, four, testing."

Bernie rewound the reels again and replayed our conversation as well as Ian's counting. Ian seemed amazed and looked at us for confirmation. Bernie rewound and replayed it again, and Ian finally spoke. "This is wonderful. Truly." He thought a moment and continued, "I'd like Oswald and Tony to try it too."

Bernie and I glanced at each other, and I was pleased at having brought the technology of the West to rural Africa. Seeing them excited with something so commonplace in our world was simply fun.

"Come on, Oswald. You try it," I said.

"No, no. I don't like these things," he answered me simply.

"Go ahead. It can't hurt," I persisted.

"No, I really do not think."

Finally Ian said, "Come on, Oswald. Speak into the machine." And so with a little coaxing, Oswald took the microphone.

He spoke. "I am Oswald Ndovi. I am the agricultural officer in this place, Ntcheu. I come from the area of Rhumpi to the north of this country of Malawi." He stopped.

It was a nice speech, and Bernie played it back to the pleasure of all of us. Oswald seemed particularly delighted.

"Come on, Tony," I said. "Let's hear you speak."

"No, I don't think I will do this," he said.

"Oh, come on."

"No, I do not think. It is very good to hear the others, but I do not think I will speak."

Bernie and I did not press him further. It was an awkward thing to request of people, and his reluctance was obviously genuine. I could not help wondering if it was the technology that made him hesitate or just the awkwardness of the moment, or was it something that was regarded as magical, or was it witchcraft even? The tapes, after all, now contained the voice of someone: sounds of a living creature were now in a machine. Could it harm a person if his voice was now separated from him and was controlled by another man? It was easy to understand that this was outside one's usual experience, and so I stopped.

"Would you guys like to say anything else? Try it again?" Bernie asked.

"No, no. This is enough for us." Ian spoke for himself and his friends and thanked us, and shortly the three of them departed.

Suddenly we could hear them laughing, and great gales of laughter—high-pitched giggles mixed with deep belly laughs, the type of laughing that shakes the whole body and brings tears—flooded from their room. Then there would be a moment of silence after one of them attempted to speak, his voice rushing to get the words out before laughter choked him off.

Bernie and I giggled a little too. Their laughter was infectious, and we were happy the machine brought them so much pleasure.

"Boy, they were really amazed by the recorder, weren't they, Bern?"

"I'll say. Guess if you've never seen one, it really is kind of amazing."

"I know. And wasn't it funny how Tony would have nothing to do with it?" I went on. "Listen to those guys. They must be thinking this is the eighth wonder of the world."

When the laughing at last subsided, we decided to sleep. In minutes we had readied ourselves for bed, pulled down our mosquito nets, and turned out the lantern. We had survived the first day.

I awoke to the sound of someone washing clothes in the bathtub. It was Jordan, I soon realized. He had come in while we were still asleep.

I glanced at my watch: 6:15 A.M. An early time to start the day, but Jordan was obviously eager. I leaned up on my elbow, "Jordan, that you?"

"Yes, bwana." He came to the door to answer. He smiled too.

"How are you doing?"

"Very well, sir. How did you sleep?"

"*Ndagona bwino* [I slept well]," I said deliberately, practicing my Chichewa.

"Oh, very good, sir. You speak Chichewa too beautiful."

"I sure do." I chuckled and untucked the mosquito net and swung around and stood. I grabbed my pants and put them on.

Jordan had his shirt off and was wearing gray shorts and a white T-shirt, the kind with the narrow straps over the shoulders. His forehead and arms were shining with perspiration. Washing clothes by hand is something I had not seen done since I was a child, and obviously it took considerable effort.

"Been washing, huh?" I said to keep the conversation going.

"Yes, my boss."

"That's good, but there's no rush."

"Yes, I am knowing. But I am thinking to start my duties."

"Whatever you want."

Jordan hesitated, then asked, "Do my bwanas wish the breakfast now?"

I glanced over at Bernie, who was about to get up. "That would be good," I said.

"Very good. I can do this." He was gone in a moment to make us our first meal.

As Bernie and I readied ourselves for the day ahead, we could hear the table being set by Jordan and the rest house cook. Finally, Jordan called out, "It is ready, my bosses, if you wish the breakfast now."

We sat down at the big table. Tony and Oswald had gone. The day of agricultural workers must start very early.

Jordan seemed anxious as he presented us fried eggs and toast and coffee. The rest house cook stood quietly, almost invisibly, in the little sitting room, holding the tin of margarine and the jar of peanut butter. Jordan spoke to him with great authority to bring the items forward. It was obvious that Jordan had established the chain of command. He was the top man, our personal servant, and the cook was here to serve us and Jordan too. Jordan did not thank him for responding and simply dismissed him with a few words. The cook turned and was gone, probably relieved to be free of us all.

"Did you have some coffee, Jordan?" Bernie asked.

"No, sir. I am not having."

"Would you like some?" Bernie asked again.

Jordan hesitated. "Well, yes, I can, sir," he answered cautiously.

"Good. Go get some and sit down. Have something to eat with us," I said.

"That is OK, my bwanas. I can take the coffee to the kitchen."

"No. Come and sit down," I insisted.

He hesitated. "Well, I can do so." He turned and walked out to the kitchen and was soon back with coffee in a tin cup. He pulled out a chair at the end of the table and sat down.

"Why don't you have some toast?" Bernie continued.

"If you say, my boss."

"Yes, let's make some more toast," I said.

"You are wishing more toast?" Jordan asked.

"Yes, let's get some more," I answered.

"I can do this."

"No, let's ask the cook to make it. Can't he do it?" I continued. "You sit. Look I'll check with him." I stood and walked to the outside door and yelled in the direction of the kitchen. "Bambo."

The cook jumped from the door of the blackened kitchen.

"Bwana?" He seemed anxious.

"Will you make some more toast for us?" I asked politely.

"Toasti?"

"Yes, make five or six more slices of toast—OK?" He did not respond, so I repeated it again, slowly.

"Ah, toasti." He heard a familiar word.

"That's right, toast. Can you make some toast?"

"Toasti, bwana." Obviously he was confused, and Jordan came to the door to help me and translated my request. The cook seemed relieved and quickly disappeared into his kitchen.

"Thanks, Jordan. I didn't say that very well."

"It is no trouble. These cooks such as these, they cannot speak the good English." Jordan defended my lack of skill and blamed the cook.

At the table I asked Jordan how the cook made the toast. He looked confused at first but smiled and said, "Without electricity, boss, the man simply slices the bread and then places it over the fire until it is brown."

"Of course. Sounds simple when you explain it."

"Yes, it is so." Jordan let my simple-minded question pass.

Jordan sipped his coffee and began to eat the toast that was still before us. We discussed our evening, and the conversation stayed simple. We asked Jordan how his accommodations were, how he spent the evening, what the stores were like in Mphate, how we could get to his village, and would he take us there. The cook brought the toast, and Jordan ate all of it.

We then made plans to walk to the shops after lunch and instructed Jordan that peanut butter sandwiches would be a sufficient meal. Jordan wanted to do more and assured us that he was a good cook, but we insisted.

"Well, Jordan, we're off." I spoke as I stood. "Maybe after lunch we can walk to the stores as you mentioned."

The sun was bright, and the dry-season heat, even at this early hour, was already uncomfortable. We walked to the edge of the road on which we had so foolishly struggled the night before to begin our short walk back to the boma. A small white Morris station wagon pulled alongside us.

It was Ian. He offered us a ride, which we accepted.

Bernie got into the front seat, and I climbed into the back of the four-door car. As we started off, Bernie asked Ian to take us to the hospital and introduce us around. He readily agreed.

Our ride was a short one, less than three hundred yards. We turned down a little dirt road in the opposite direction from where Gene and Dan lived and then took another right. Here were some twenty small brick houses placed closely together on each side of the dusty road that led to the hospital at the far end. Ian stopped at the first one on the right.

"Incidentally, this is your house," he said, as he smiled.

I did not like what I saw. The house was fifteen feet long at most and maybe ten feet in depth. There was no grass, no trees or bushes, and it was about ten feet from the house next to it. It was old, plain, rundown, and bleak.

"How do you like it?"

"It seems OK," Bernie said. I detected a shakiness in his voice.

"Come. I'll show you around," Ian said as he stepped from the car. "These are the houses for the junior medical staff. This is the one we are going to make ready for you."

We followed him across the bare ground that led to the front door. I was numbed. The house was so tiny that I could not imagine the three of us squeezing into it. The prospect of actually living there was inconceivable.

Ian knocked on the door. "*Odi* [Hello. A greeting announcing one's arrival at someone's doorstep]," he shouted out.

"*Odini* [Hello. Come in]." A woman's voice came from the far side of the house.

Ian turned the doorknob slowly and pushed the door gently forward. "Odi," he said once again.

"Odini, bwana." The woman, standing in the back courtyard could now see us through the back door of the house, and she invited us again.

Ian stepped forward and we followed him. It was a shock. I had been in the country for over a week and had seen hundreds of small houses. But this was the first time I had actually been in one. The room must have been eight feet by eight feet, ten by ten at the most. This was the living room.

As Bernie and I stood silently, trying to comprehend what was happening, Ian opened another little door. Here was the second room, nearly the same, but without the doors that led to the outside. This was the bedroom, and we could see straw mats on the floor where the family slept.

"Well, that's the tour," Ian said. "Doesn't take long." He tried to be serious, but he asked, "What is that expression you have? A man's home is his castle? Something like that?"

"Yes, that's it," Bernie answered without a hint of enjoyment in his voice. I said nothing.

"Well, you have one of the littlest castles in all the world." He smiled and stepped quickly into the small courtyard at the back.

Two women and five little children were standing at attention when Bernie and I stepped outside. The kids stared at us intently and would not take their eyes from us. We were probably among the first white people they had seen and maybe the first they had ever seen so closely, and their stares were understandable. I found their obvious amazement to be amusing and winked at one of the little girls, who blushed.

Ian introduced us, and we shook hands with the women and all the children. He then pointed to the back wall of the courtyard and explained that the door on the right was for the *chimbudzi* [latrine] and the doorway on the left was the cooking room in the rainy season. In the middle was another doorway where a sink belonged. This family used it for storage, and I could see a large burlap bag nearly full of what I assumed was maize. Ian said, "Right now there is no water at this place, but we will run a waterline into this little room. This should make things easier for you."

There was nothing else to see. We stood awkwardly, trying to take some comfort in the fact that we were so privileged as to have our own water supply on the premises.

Ian said we could be going, and we agreed and bade farewell to the women and children and quickly walked back to Ian's car.

"Well, how'd you like it?" He smiled again as he spoke.

"It's OK, I guess," Bernie repeated his initial comment.

"You know, you chaps can put all your katundu in one room. You have so much. Then you can sleep in the other room."

It was funny and true, but neither of us laughed. We thought we had very few possessions; yet compared to the current occupants, we were ridiculously overburdened, and I wondered if we could get two beds and a table and chairs to fit into the house along with everything else.

Ian seemed to sense that our concern was legitimate, at least from our perspective. He said, "Oh, it is a very tiny place indeed. I told the people in Blantyre it was no good for you. But these Peace Corps people, they kept insisting."

"What did they insist?" I asked.

"That you live just like a health worker, one of these junior health assistants." He turned back toward me and continued, "There is one more problem. I have no place for this family here. They will be moving to a village just close to the boma."

"You mean when we move in, these people have no place to live?" I asked with surprise.

"That is correct," Ian said.

"We kick a family out so we can move in," Bernie summed up. His voice reflected his disbelief. It was a shocking prospect. We had come to help out at this rural hospital, and on our first day we must dislocate a family.

As we started to get into the car, we saw Dan riding toward us on a bicycle. He dismounted and quickly greeted us and shook Ian's hand. He said he was on his way to teach a math class and was late. He explained that he and Gene had talked after our visit and decided that it would make sense if we moved in with them, as they had a spare bedroom. Without hesitation Bernie and I accepted, and the issue of our little house was resolved immediately. Ian was delighted with the invitation too and told Dan so. We chatted for a few minutes and Dan departed, leaving all of us pleased.

Ian then reached into the side pocket of his jacket and removed his car keys. He walked to the back of the little car, Bernie and I following him. "Now that we have solved the housing problem, I think I'll give this family a gift for their troubles. We do not get fresh fish often and I purchased some extras this morning at the market." Ian lifted the back door up into the air and reached in toward some newspapers.

Bernie turned quickly toward me. He looked directly at me, his eyes opened wide, showing excitement, and then he looked down at the back section of the car.

I leaned forward and looked down. There it was, a tape recorder. I was speechless, frozen and embarrassed. I did not know what to say. We must have seemed so arrogant with our technology of the West, but we were made the fools. Their great gales of laughter were all at our expense, and it was humiliating to think how we had behaved. What had we been thinking? We surely had failed their test.

It was a lesson I would never forget. We were the arrogant know-it-alls, superior with our technology, our culture, actually. "We" credited "them" with little experience or exposure to the modern world, our world, the world that supposedly mattered. They were the teachers this time, a bit severe, perhaps, but painfully effective. The technology was universal, available to anyone with money. Our superior financial positions were simply the result of our birthplace, and they knew this. We had now been initiated into Africa.

Ian removed some of the newspapers and one fish and said nothing.

Chapter Four

Introduction to Misery

We stepped onto the covered khonde of the administration building as a door suddenly opened on our right. Out stepped a distinguished-looking man. He had white hair and wore a short white lab coat, and he greeted us with a big smile.

"Hello, I am Misomali." He extended his hand to each of us, and we in turn introduced ourselves. Misomali continued, "So you are the new Peace Corps volunteers who have come to work on the tuberculosis project."

"Yes, we are," Bernie replied.

"Ah, this is very good. We have so much TB here."

"That's what we are told," Bernie continued.

"Anything you can do will help us." Misomali then asked, "And just what will you be doing?"

"Well, we hope to be working in the villages near the boma, to do some survey work and to do some Mantoux tests. Then people will put together some statistics on tuberculosis. Basically, we hope to be able to treat people but we want to study the disease, too," I said.

"I see. This is a very good thing," Misomali replied.

"We hope so," I answered. "There are some people in Blantyre and at a university in the United States who are experts on this disease, and our job is to produce some data for these people to analyze."

"And where will you put the sick people?" he asked.

"We hope to keep them in the villages. One of the things we are trying to do is to find people with TB and then to treat them in their homes so that we do not have to use hospital facilities," I responded.

"I see."

Then Bernie asked, "And what do you do with TB patients now?"

"Well, it is very difficult with these people, you know. We just try to do what we can." Misomali seemed a little embarrassed with this reply, as if the shortcomings of the Malawian health system were somehow his own.

"I see," Bernie answered. "But do you bring them into the hospital?"

"Yes, we can. We have some here. But it is very sad, though. You see, there is very little we can do for them," Misomali answered tenderly, and I could begin to see in his remark just how difficult and frustrating his job must be. His ability to endure in such a setting went, I assumed, largely unrecognized; but it was a testament to his humanity to never stop struggling, or so it seemed.

"Do you have a TB ward for these people?" Bernie asked.

"I am afraid we do not. They just stay with the other patients."

"You mean you just mix the TB patients in with everyone else?" Bernie restated Misomali's remark.

"I am afraid this is true. You see we have very little room here. And so we do the best we can."

I knew this was often the case because Malawi would need sanitariums throughout the country if it was to combat even this one disease. The reality of hearing this was somehow still shocking, since now I had to actually deal with it.

"And so, how are you settling in?" Misomali changed the topic.

"We're doing fine. So far, so good," I answered. I then explained that we would not be living in the small hospital house that was selected for us but rather would be staying with the teachers. Misomali was obviously pleased and stated that this would be better for everyone. He then asked if we would like a tour of the hospital.

We said we would, and Misomali turned and led us into his office. It was large and clean and all white, but nearly empty, containing a desk and chair, an examination table, a screen, and one large bookcase with four old books and some papers.

"This is my place. I do the examinations and the administration work here," Misomali informed us.

"Do you see all the people who come here?" I asked.

"No. I see only just some of the people. You see there on the lower side we have the outpatients. Perhaps you saw the long line of people when you came in. These people go to the outpatient area. If they are very sick, they come to see me. So I do not see many people. And, of course, I must do the operations."

"Who sees the outpatients?" Bernie asked.

"They are the health assistants. They see the people and then the patients come to me or to my assistant, Mr. Chumia, whom you will meet." Misomali smiled anxiously and suggested we start the tour. "Come, I will introduce you to my clerk."

We followed him to a small adjoining office and walked directly inside. A man in a suit and tie stood up quickly and came to attention. "This is Mr. Nyirenda, our senior clerk here. He does the records and the books for the hospital." We were introduced and greeted politely but soon were on our way.

Misomali removed a key from his pocket and quickly opened the door next to Mr. Nyirenda's office, and we stepped inside. It was a terrible sight. Boxes were all over the room, some opened, some still closed, many stacked on one another. Supplies were scattered everywhere—bandages, crutches, pills, sheets, and bottles of strange concoctions. It appeared to be total confusion.

"These are our hospital supplies. Only Mr. Nyirenda and I have the key to this storeroom. I am afraid it is a bit messy, but someday we must take the time to get it organized. I am afraid Mr. Nyirenda does not have the time."

"Perhaps Bruce and I could fix up the place this week, since we will have little to do at first," Bernie offered.

"That will be very good if you can. Then we will know how many supplies we have. You see, it is a problem for us to know when to order things." Misomali's comment seemed genuine, but its implication panicked me. I wondered how often they ran out of things, even available things, and how much unnecessary suffering took place because the system was so unformed.

Misomali turned and led us out. He locked the door, and we proceeded quickly up a small hill to the only ward of the hospital.

Some patients were sitting on a worn-out patch of grass. Several of them were weaving straw mats. Some were bandaged; some simply looked very ill. They glanced toward us but said nothing.

We went up a short flight of stairs and stepped under the hospital's large overhanging iron roof, where we found twenty or more people—some asleep, some sitting with their backs against the building, their eyes without focus.

"Do these people come out here during the day to get some fresh air?" Bernie asked.

"Yes, some can. But for most, they sleep here at night. You see, these wards are too crowded, so some must sleep on little mats outside." Misomali's reply was straightforward, and he stepped quickly inside the ward.

It was a nightmarish scene, and it overwhelmed me. I could make no comparisons to anything I had seen or read before. Men were everywhere, on the beds, under the beds, in the aisles between the beds, a few wandering about listlessly. While several slept and seemed peaceful and a few were being attended to by the health assistants, most did nothing, and so the ward seemed to be a cage for storing and stacking sick bodies, as in a concentration camp. These were not complete men anymore. They were rodents, perhaps, confined and piled on each other, waiting for extermination when their bodies deteriorated just a bit more.

But it was the odor, the odor of their bodies, that devastated me. It was offensive, sour and rank, and it seeped into my head and onto my skin and clothes. It physically connected me to them. Their wretched bodies now touched mine, and I was not simply looking at them but was joined with them. Needing to breathe, I could not escape them.

Bernie was as obviously troubled as I by the experience. His face was expressionless as he tried to comprehend the experience of these wretched men, and yet his eyes were intense as he looked from one body to the next. Finally, Bernie spoke, "What's this man in here for?" He nodded to a man lying on top of the bed near Misomali.

"I do not know." There was no name or any medical record on the bed to which Misomali could refer, and so he turned and called out to one of the health assistants, who quickly came to him. Misomali spoke in Chichewa and asked what the man's troubles were. The health assistant stepped alongside the bed and spoke gently to the sick man. I wondered whether he was asking the patient about his ailments or if he perhaps just wanted to know his name.

The health assistant straightened up and reported to his boss. Misomali then informed us that the man had pains in his chest, perhaps in his lungs.

"Are there some records we could see?" I asked Misomali.

"Yes, there should be," Misomali answered and then directed the health assistant to bring the medical records.

The health assistant walked quickly to a large table at the end of the ward. Another assistant joined him, and the two started sorting through a large stack of metal clipboards that were haphazardly thrown on the table. They were having problems locating the man's records, and finally the first assistant returned to the bed, and I could hear him ask the sick man his name.

He returned again to the table and joined his colleague in trying to locate the records. Their problems were obvious to me. They had perhaps a hundred men in the ward, and there were fewer than twenty-five clipboards. So each clipboard must have contained multiple sets of records. The lack of order in the ward was as obvious here as it had been in the storage room. I tried to withhold judgment since it seemed unfair for an outsider who had not worked in this hellish place to be critical, but I knew that without a reasonable record system there was little hope of helping anyone. I said nothing as the three of us waited, but my shock was obvious to Misomali, and he was visibly embarrassed.

At last the health assistant came to us and handed Misomali the clipboard. Misomali spoke to him softly and the assistant reached out and flipped up some scraps of papers under the metal clip until he stopped at the patient's sheet.

"Blaki Wiskasi," Misomali read the name from the top of the simple form.

"Ah, bwana," the health assistant indicated this was the man.

"Blaki Wiskasi," Misomali read the name again, his voice pitched higher to indicate his skepticism. Quickly he stepped forward and asked the sick man his name. The reply I heard imperfectly, but it sounded like Chibambo.

Misomali did not hesitate but asked again. Was he Mr. Chibambo or Mr. Blaki Wiskasi? The sick man indicated he was both, and Misomali seemed satisfied.

Misomali then handed me the chart and I glanced down at a nearly blank page. At the top was written "Blaki Wiskasi"; in the center was written "pains to the chest." The man's complaints, it seemed, were simply copied on the paper, and this now appeared to be the agreed-upon diagnosis.

"Do you know anything?" Bernie asked. "Do you think it's his heart or his lungs? Maybe it's cancer or maybe even TB," he continued.

"Yes. It could be these things. But we do not know," Misomali answered.

"Have you done any tests or had him x-rayed?" Bernie continued.

Misomali turned to the health assistant and, using a mixture of English and Chichewa, asked what tests had been given and what was being done for this man. The health assistant paused and thought. Then he reached over and took the chart back from Misomali and looked at the medical form. He began to rapidly flip over the pages until he discovered a small piece of paper, inserted in with those of another patient, and this gave him his answer. "The man is just resting now," he finally said.

Misomali took the chart and looked at the scrap of paper. I glanced over and saw the man's name and the simple directions written in pencil, "x-ray."

"So this man is to go for x-ray?" Misomali asked.

"Yes, bwana."

"Where do they go for x-rays?" Bernie asked.

"They go to Zomba Hospital," Misomali replied.

"How far's that?" Bernie asked.

"Some eighty miles."

"How do they get there?" I asked.

"By the hospital vehicle. We can take five or six. We go approximately every two weeks."

"Who reads the x-rays?" Bernie asked.

"We get them here. Then we send them and the medical information to the Queen Elizabeth Hospital in Blantyre, and the doctor there reads them. Then the information is sent to us."

"So this man is just waiting then to go to Zomba," I stated the obvious.

"Yes, it seems to be so," Misomali answered.

"Isn't he receiving any medication?" I asked.

Misomali translated my question to the health assistant who was at a loss for an answer. Finally he turned to the other health assistant, who had quietly come over to listen to our conversation. He spoke rapidly in Chichewa to him, trying to get his answer. I heard the word *penicillin* mentioned as they conversed, and the health assistant finally gave us the answer. "He is having penicillin."

Misomali stared at him for a moment, then repeated, "Penicillin."

"Yes, bwana," the health assistant replied.

"How many times?"

"*T.I.D.*," [Three times daily] the health assistant answered.

Misomali was obviously unsatisfied with the answer, and he stepped alongside the sick man and spoke to him. My Chichewa did not allow me to follow, but Misomali seemed to ask him whether he had received any medicine today. The sick man said no. Misomali asked if he received any medicine yesterday. Again the man said no.

It was a frightening and embarrassing situation. Misomali became rigid but said nothing. The two health assistants looked to other patients while Bernie and I slowly twisted our bodies to relieve a little tension. Obviously, nothing was being done for the man, and he might even be better off staying in his own village, where he would be with his family. No diagnosis had been made, and it was not clear when one would be made. The record system was hopeless and if any medicines were dispensed at all, they were administered sporadically and with little thought to their impact. I wondered whether the entire hospital was operating this poorly. Could it be that only illnesses that would cure themselves anyway were the successes of this place and that all the seriously ill were doomed? This pathetic cluster of buildings was meant to serve the district's 300,000 people, but it would be a wonder if it served anyone at all.

Misomali indicated that we should be going. Perhaps he hoped we had not understood, perhaps he was simply resigned to the inefficiency, or perhaps he needed to psychologically protect himself. And so he walked away.

The women's ward was on the other end of this long, rectangular building, and it was to be our next stop. Misomali, Bernie, and I exited on the far side of the building and walked along the outside of the ward. Once again we passed about a dozen men and women who were huddled alongside. We stopped at the open doorway to the women's ward, and Misomali stepped just inside the door, leaving us on the walkway. A female health assistant, perhaps twenty years of age, came over, knelt down on both knees before him, and reached up to shake his hand while she greeted him. This was a display of extreme respect, I knew, but it seemed inappropriate outside a village setting; and it made me suspect that Misomali rarely came here.

We were introduced to the young woman, who remained kneeling as we shook her hand. Technically, she was our counterpart, our equal, but this was such a fiction that we just let the greeting play out in the manner she thought appropriate.

Misomali did not invite us in at first. The ward was so crowded that it would have been difficult for us to walk around. He explained that healthy mothers often accompanied their sick children to the hospital and stayed with them and that healthy small children often accompanied their sick mothers. This meant that on nearly every bed and on every mattress pad on the floor under the beds there were two people, or three, or even four if a mother had additional youngsters in tow. As I looked in, I had the impression of a human anthill—some creatures climbing atop each other, some huddled in little niches to avoid being bumped or stepped on. Were the listless movements of the women and children due to their illness, or were these poor souls so stripped of their dignity that they retreated to some simpler life form, perhaps still with compassion for one another but lacking in hope for themselves? It was a scene that numbed me even more than what I had seen in the men's ward, and I could see Bernie was affected this way too.

Suddenly, Misomali saw something, and he walked quickly inside to a bed at the far end of the ward. We followed but quickly learned that we should have stayed outside. A small girl of about eight years of age was bent over one of the cots, her upper body resting on the mattress, her hips and legs dangling to the floor, her toes just touching the concrete. She was naked and her legs, particularly the inner thighs, above the knees were severely burned. She seemed in terrible pain and she cried, whimpered actually, and seemed not to notice us as she tried to escape into sleep.

Misomali was very disturbed. He asked some questions of the young health assistant, who did nothing but shake his head.

"When did this happen?" Bernie asked.

"She came three days ago. The parents carried her from the village," Misomali answered.

"How did it happen?" Bernie went on.

"You know these village people. They sleep near the *nyumba* [the huts]. Sometimes they have a small fire, and the people sleep too close to it. This girl's clothing caught fire while sleeping. She may have rolled into the fire. This sometimes happens." He paused and added, "But this is the hot season, so I do not know why they had the fire. It is too sad."

"What's being done for her?" I asked.

Misomali hesitated. "Well, we have no morphine." He stopped. He waited. "You see, the morphine is finished, so there is little we can do to help her. She is taking aspirin and nutrition. And we gave her antibiotics for the infection."

"You mean she's just there suffering? There's no way to help relieve the pain?" My reply was quick. My disbelief filled my voice until it trembled. I went on, "This is horrible, Misomali. She's just suffering. We must do something. There must be something else we can give her."

"I am sorry, but there is nothing we can do. She is so exhausted now that she is even sleeping a bit. So this is good. I think she may live if the infection does not come. This is how the things go here."

Bernie spoke, "But can't we drive to another hospital and get some morphine? Can't we go to Blantyre?"

"I am sorry, but we cannot do this. We have no money, and the ambulance is at the shop to this time. I will call the central medical stores, and they will send a packet with the morphine. It will come by bus, and so we must wait."

"But when will it come?" Bernie pleaded.

"It will come soon, and then we will give it to her."

"Could we go to Blantyre to get it?" Bernie asked.

"This could be, but it should take you two days. We can wait for the bus." Misomali said a few words to the health assistant and then spoke to us, "This is very sad but this is how the things go here." He then walked from the girl and out into the sunshine and we followed, having done nothing.

Bernie and I were distraught, drained. Our bodies were as listless as those of the patients themselves. This last scene and our inability to help someone in such pain was beyond our experience and our imagination. We stopped outside Misomali's office and told him we must be going for the day. I suspected he could see how upset we were, but he was amazingly cheerful and smiled and wished us well. Was he showing us that this was a place of sadness and that we should learn to deal with it because that is how things go here?

Chapter Five

Small Talk: Good Lessons

"Jordan, how many sugars do you want?" I called out.

"I can have five, boss," he shouted back.

"That all?" I smiled as I started spooning the sugar into his coffee cup. "How about ten, like Robert over here?"

Robert was sitting across from me at our dining-room table in the large house which Mike Hill and I now shared with Dan and Bastone. His back was to the large window that overlooked the little chicken house and the fields of maize beyond them, and he smiled and protested. "No, boss, I did not have ten spoons. I take six only, sure."

"Bullshit, Robert. You filled the cup with sugar and then poured in a little coffee. I saw you." Once again I was poking fun at Robert, and as usual he was taking it in his own good-natured way. "Don't they have any sugar over at your house? Jordan tells me you eat two pounds of sugar over here every week. And someday you're going to turn into a fat bastard."

Robert shook his head in protest, although I was not sure he completely understood me. Jordan came through the door of the kitchen, his face beaming, "Fat bastard, boss. My dear Robert a fat bastard. No, this cannot be." With this said, he began to laugh loudly and to clap his hands and stamp his bare feet on the concrete floor. He pointed to Robert and though his words were still mixed with laughter he asked, "*Achimwene, mwamva* [Friend, do you understand]? Fat bastard."

Robert mumbled something in Chichewa indicating that his understanding was incomplete, and so Jordan began an animated explanation of my comment. It was funny to hear him speak and

47

laugh simultaneously while inserting the words *fat bastard* whenever necessary. The more he explained, the more he laughed; and soon Robert and I were laughing along with him.

Robert kept protesting even as he laughed, and I wondered if singling someone out for the amusement of others was commonplace in Malawian villages. I guessed it was. Almost all the Malawians I had met loved to laugh, and it just seemed like something human beings everywhere must do. I wondered too how Jordan translated *bastard* and hoped that he had not been too literal. My Chichewa, after a year in Malawi, allowed me to operate reasonably well on my own in the villages where I could control the conversation and most of the vocabulary, but this was beyond my capacity. Jordan, true to his word, had remarkable language skills, and so I hoped he caught the nuances of this playful expression.

Jordan calmed down and joined Robert and me at the table. The three of us generally had coffee together each morning after the others had gone off to work. Gene had left some seven months earlier and Bernie, who had a master's degree in hospital administration and who wanted to work in the Queen Elizabeth Hospital in Blantyre, had switched positions with Mike Hill, who wanted to live in a rural area. Dan was still here and Bastone had moved back in, although he lived somewhat separately from us, doing his own laundry and cooking his own food on a little kerosene stove he set up in his bedroom.

Our little community of *azungu* [Europeans or Caucasians] had grown too. Three new volunteers, John Dixon, John Devendorff, and Dave Bush, had joined the teaching staff at the secondary school and they, along with an eighteen-year-old fellow from Bristol, England, Bob Wigmore, who taught with them, moved into a new house in our little complex. Robert had become their cook although they were now in the process of looking for someone else.

We sat for a few minutes sipping coffee. I jumped up and pulled the top of my shorts down a few inches and stuck out my stomach as far as I could. "Yeah, Robert, you're going to have a big *mimba* like this in a couple of years." Then I strutted around the room trying to make myself as puffed up and fat looking as I could. Robert and Jordan burst into laughter again. Play acting or mimicking anyone, I had learned, was a guaranteed laugh, and they did not let me down. They howled with approval. It was silly business, barely slapstick, but everybody loved it and we had fun.

When I sat down and gained control, I asked them what the expression was for a pregnant woman.

"Pregnant, boss?" Jordan inquired.

"Yeah, how do you say someone's pregnant? I heard someone

at the hospital use the expression, and I wasn't sure what it was."

"Oh, boss, it's '*mkazi wa mimba*'," Jordan said and Robert nodded in agreement.

"Oh, I see. Woman with stomach. Right?"

"Yes, boss. That is it."

"So, Robert will be *munthu wa mimba yaikulu*, if he keeps eating all this sugar."

Jordan burst into laughter again. "Munthu wa mimba yaikulu," he screamed. "My Robert. Munthu wa mimba yaikulu. No, boss, no, no. This cannot be." He could hardly speak. It was a ridiculous expression, almost outrageous, and through his laughter he tried to explain to Robert my new joke. The image of Robert as the pregnant man thoroughly broke them up and I, while hoping they were not offended, was thoroughly enjoying them.

I knew I could go on with these word games as I so often did, but instead I asked, "Say, do you know about the magic roots?"

"The what, boss?" Jordan asked.

"The magic roots," I said.

"What is this? I do not understand." Jordan looked at me seriously and then looked to Robert for help. His forehead and eyes indicated he was trying to understand.

"You know, magic roots," I said. "I heard that if a woman did not want a baby, she would tie some kind of roots around her waist and she wouldn't get pregnant."

Jordan stared at me and then spoke to Robert. They both seemed a little embarrassed, and Robert lowered his eyes. Jordan said, "How did you learn this, boss?"

"Hey, I've been around. I've learned a few things. I heard that if a woman tied a string around her waist and then hung a special kind of root off each hip, she would not get pregnant. Now is this true?"

Jordan again spoke softly to Robert. He turned back to me and said, "This can be, boss. This is so."

"So these roots work then? I mean the people think these roots work?" I asked.

"Yes, boss, they can work."

"Well, what kind of root are they? Where do you get them?"

Jordan spoke to Robert. I could see Robert shaking his head and Jordan trying to come up with an answer. Finally, he said, "I cannot know these things. The women to the village know of this. Where to get this root. It is not for us the men to know."

"But they work?" I asked.

"Oh, yes, boss. This I know to be true. These are very powerful roots." Jordan hesitated and then asked, "Why do you want to know these things, my bwana?"

"So I can get a big pile of them. I have a lot of girlfriends, you know."

"You want the roots, boss, for the girlfriends. Is this so?" Jordan seemed amazed, but slowly a large smile overcame his face. He said, "You are teasing me again, boss."

"Well, maybe I am, but I am interested in this type of thing."

"You are interested to the African medicine? Why is this?" Jordan asked.

"Well, because I want to know how it works. I mean it must work or people would not go to the *sing'anga* [healer or traditional doctor]. Right?"

"This is true. These men can cure too many of the diseases. They are clever to the curing, this I know." Jordan turned to Robert for confirmation. He spoke in Chichewa to explain our conversation, and Robert, who was paying careful attention, finally nodded in agreement.

"But, I am just thinking it can only be for us Africans and not for the Europeans." Then Jordan asked, "Do the people of America have doctors such as these sing'angas?"

"Well, yes, I guess so. I mean most people go to the regular doctors and get *mankhwala* [medicine] or have operations, but some people say prayers too. And some people say they can cure you if they touch you or if you believe they have the power." My explanation was accurate, I guessed, but so brief that I felt silly. Oddly, I realized that Jordan was more tolerant of our medicine with its mixture of science and supernatural components than most Westerners were of his medicine. Few people I knew would ever credit a witch doctor's machinations with being anything more than mumbo-jumbo mixed with a little psychological suggestion, while they would take seriously someone's claim that prayer to the Judeo-Christian God had brought about a cure. Our prejudices were clear to me, and I guessed that because these village people had black skin and appeared to us so simple, few of us could see the similarities in our lives—that all people had illnesses and took steps to handle them, that all people sought control, and that people were rational and got results from health practitioners or they would not go back to them. The fact that some of the traditional medicines could be efficacious and that bone setting and rest were obvious, rational forms of curing were generally overlooked in the search for the bizarre.

I continued, "So in some ways the systems are similar except we have more trained doctors, doctors trained at universities anyway." I then asked, "Do you go to the sing'anga, Jordan?"

"Yes, I do. They can be too powerful for the illnesses."

"Do you go to the *chipatala* [hospital] here in the boma too?" I knew people generally used both traditional and Western medicine in some combination so as to maximize their chances, and I wondered if my clever friend followed this pattern.

"Well, yes. I can go to hospital here. My Ida takes the kids to the shots and such as that."

"Did you ever stay at the hospital?" I continued.

"No, boss. This is no good place. I do not like." He paused and thought. "It is a filthy place, boss."

"What about Ida? Where did she have all the kids?"

"She is having the babies to the village. The old women can be the midwives, and they know these things. This hospital here is no good to this matter. It is better to the villages."

I understood completely. Although I spent most of my time in the last year in the villages surrounding the boma, Mike and I generally spent our mornings at the hospital doing our lab work and helping out in any way we could. While we had made a little headway in improving the record system in the wards, and the storeroom and pharmacy were now reasonably well organized, the hospital itself remained a sorry place.

I began to ask another question when Jordan spoke again. "You see at this time, boss, the sister to my Ida is having the new baby to the hospital. I should say, the baby was born three days ago to the village but the little boy is too sick."

"What's the matter? Is he there now?" I asked.

"Yes, they came in the night and the child and the mother are there to this time. Ida's going there too early this morning," Jordan answered.

"Well, what's the trouble?" I asked again.

Jordan hesitated, choosing his words carefully. "Well, my bwana, there is no hole for the *tudzi*, the shit, to come out."

"What?"

"There is no hole for the shit to come." Jordan was concerned and his voice was strained.

"What are you saying? There's no asshole? This kid doesn't have an asshole?" I was incredulous, confused.

"Yes, boss. This seems to be the situation." Jordan then went into a long explanation for Robert, and Robert shook his head softly and said, "*Pepani, pepani* [Sorry, sorry],"—indicating his sympathy with this horrible prospect.

"This can't be, Jordan. I mean I've never heard of such a thing. Everyone's got an asshole," I protested. "Are you sure you're right?"

"Well, the mother says there is no *tudzi* to this time. And the people can see no hole. So this is how it seems," Jordan said.

"Has the baby seen Misomali?" I asked.

"I am not knowing this, my boss, for Ida has not returned."

"Well, I'll check it out when I go over there. I'll make sure Misomali sees the baby. Maybe they could send the kid to Blantyre to have an operation or something." I offered my help but knew if such a thing was possible, the chances for the baby's survival were small indeed. I asked Jordan the child's name.

"The child is having no name to this time," Jordan informed me. "You see, boss, in the villages the people do not give the babies names for some time."

I remembered someone explaining to me how newborns were often not named for several weeks so that the parents could be reasonably sure they would live. With infant mortality so high, it seemed people were reluctant to give full recognition to the humanity of the infant and therefore withheld a name. If true, this was certainly different than a Western view of children who were regarded, at least in recent centuries, as fully enfranchised with human qualities and rights at birth, or even before birth. The Malawians' resistence to naming children quickly was an oddly rational action on their part and probably protected parents psychologically, especially given the considerable likelihood of an infant's not surviving. We were also similar, in some ways, I concluded. Did not our children assume a greater and more complete humanness as they got older? While both would be difficult to accept, the death of a five-year-old brought greater sadness than the death of a newborn.

"So what's the family name, the surname, then?" I asked Jordan.

"The family name?" Jordan inquired.

"Well, what's the father's name?" I had been doing census work in the villages for months, and I knew that people generally had only one name, as was done historically in Europe in earlier times.

"It is Josefu, boss."

"Just Josefu? No second name?"

"No. This is all, boss."

"What about a clan name?" I asked.

"Well, he is to my clan. He is Phiri, too."

"OK, then. I should be able to find them. I'll see what's up." I then added, "I can't believe this. This seems horrible."

Robert slowly stood up. He had finished his coffee, and he informed us that he was going back to his house to iron the laundry. It was a big task each week since the heat made us perspire a good deal, and we changed clothes frequently. Of course, the fact that we did not do our own laundry made us even more careless with our clothes.

"Ndapita, bwana," Robert said as he passed through the kitchen doorway.

"*Pitani bwino* [Go well], achimwene, Robert," I waved him good-bye and I smiled. Robert was a bit of a sadsack, possessing few of the capabilities of Jordan, but I liked him dearly, and I enjoyed our little gathering each morning.

"Say, Jordan. Who's that woman that Robert's got living with him? She's not the same one I saw him with last month, is she?"

"No, boss. This can be a new one," Jordan answered.

"Did he marry this one?"

"No, boss. It is just the girlfriend."

"Where the hell did he meet her?" Then I added with an obvious lack of charity, "She looks like a real village sweetie." Cooks and houseboys of necessity were going to marry village women with a minimum of education and experience, like Jordan's wife, Ida; and my remark was unwarranted.

Jordan let my comment pass. If he felt hurt and insulted, he did not show it, and as so often happened, the inequality in our relationship once again presented itself. I loved Jordan and respected him thoroughly for his intelligence and his many abilities, which surpassed mine in so many ways. I wondered if my insensitive comment stemmed from the fact that I was the employer and he the worker or was something deeper, such as race and education and cultural superiority. Could I have a real friendship with him if I possessed these attributes, however subtly and unconsciously they worked in me? Could he have a true friendship with me if he was simply a recipient of my largesse, something he would legitimately seek given his alternatives? It was a painful question if formulated in these stark terms—my patronizing him, his hustling me. I hoped it was more complex and that human relationships could be founded on respect and caring despite the inherent inequality of an employer-employee relationship, despite vast cultural differences. It was an important issue to me, and I wondered how the millions of people around the world in similar situations resolved it—or if they even considered it, for that matter. I was not sure I would ever know the answer, but I suspected that there would be many events through time that would test our relationship, just as happened with people claiming friendship everywhere. For now I would simply try to show more sensitivity toward Jordan and Robert.

"Well, I believe my Robert met the lady to the market," Jordan answered. "She is staying at Eneya village, boss, near to the shops at Mphate."

"Oh, I know Eneya village. Bernie and I worked there for about three months this year. I don't remember her, though."

"Well, she has come recently to this place. She is from Dedza district, close to the place of Chief Gomani, near to Fort Mlangeni.

She is having this brother to Eneya village and is remaining to his house."

"That's why I didn't meet her. Because she's just come here."

"This could be so, boss," Jordan answered simply and then sipped his coffee.

"Well, what happened to the other lady? Wasn't that his wife or something? I thought they were married."

"Well, it was just a little bit like that." Jordan hesitated but offered some details. "You know, boss, it is the traditional marriage. Robert can be just having the marriage to the village."

"You mean he didn't get it registered or get married in a church?" I asked.

Jordan nodded and said, "This is true, boss. And so my Robert has disqualified the marriage. He has instructed this lady to go away." He waited and added, "You know, boss, they had so many fights. Screaming to each other and like that. Did you hear them, boss?"

"Well, I didn't hear them. But Dixon told me they were always yelling at each other. One time he even went out to their quarters to see if everyone was OK." I added what little I knew to our juicy neighborhood domestic scandal.

"This can be, boss. Ah, it is no good."

"So she hit the trail then."

"What, boss?

"She's gone then? I mean it's over?"

"Yes, it is finished." Jordan continued with more details, "Actually she pinched the small radio of Robert and the batteries. And she is having the blanket and the new dress that Robert bought to the khonde tailors." He paused and added, "Robert is too angry and he wishes to get these items back."

"So she cleaned him out, huh? That's funny," I commented.

"It is funny, boss?" Jordan spoke quickly.

I could see that he did not think this was the least bit amusing. Again, I realized that I was out of line. I was the one who regarded the items as being so insignificant in value, who failed to see things from Robert's or Jordan's point of view. I tried to recover. "Well, I mean it's interesting. So, what's going to happen now?"

"It is a little bit complicated. Robert went to the village to speak to the brother to return the items. But this man I take to be a bad man. He cannot seem to help poor Robert. And the woman has returned to Fort Mlangeni, I should say to Lizulu, with the things."

"So old dumb Robert's screwed then." I continued, "But can't he go to the *mfumu* [headman] at the village, to Mfumu Eneya, to get things straightened out? I knew him pretty well when I worked there. He seems like a pretty reasonable guy. Can't he get a little palaver together and settle it?''

"Well, this is true. But it is a bit difficult because the woman is to another village, and Robert cannot live to Eneya village. So it is like this.''

"Oh, I see. Mfumu Eneya can't settle it unless both people are from his village?''

"Yes, it is a bit like that, boss," Jordan explained.

"So that's it then?" I said.

"Well no, boss. Robert is going to the traditional court.''

"You mean at that little brick building just to the south of here? The one off the main road?''

"Yes, that's the one," Jordan answered.

"What happens there?''

"He can argue to the chiefs there and they can decide," he explained briefly.

"What chiefs, Jordan?''

"Well, boss, they are these local chiefs here who do these things. Before the British came, the chiefs to the village made the decisions such as this and so today too. These are the traditional courts for us Africans in these matters, but not such things as the robbery or murder. And the big bwanas can go to the big courts for which I am not knowing.''

"So they just decide on small things like divorces then?" I inquired.

"Well yes, boss. But the divorce cannot just be a small thing.''

"I'm sorry, Jordan. Of course, it's not a small thing. It just sounded less complicated than real courts. I guess because there's no lawyers and fancy buildings.''

"But the divorce can be difficult, my bwana. So the chiefs must be clever.''

"So what do you think will happen in Robert's case? I mean, does he have to get divorced, too?" I asked with growing fascination and, I am afraid, some amusement.

"I cannot be knowing if he can get these items back. But the marriage can be disqualified, sure, boss.''

"They'll just cancel the marriage, huh? And will Robert have to pay some money to the woman?" I asked.

"This can be, boss. I should say that Robert can pay some five shillings and the wife she can receive one pound or one pound five. Yes, it can be like this." Jordan then added, "It is very dear the divorce these days.''

"You think it's expensive getting a divorce?" My comment was condescending, and I tried to cover it up without Jordan having to answer. I immediately asked, "I mean what's a divorce cost if there was a registered marriage?''

"Oh, this is for the big bwanas. Not for the village people such as Robert and Jordan. Oh, boss, it is too dear. This I know. But I cannot say the money. It is not for me."

"Well, I'm sorry for Robert. It sounds like a bad situation." I added, "What I cannot understand is why he's got a new girlfriend already, before he's settled with the old one."

"Well, this is the way of Robert. He can have so many girlfriends. And you know, boss, he has recently bought this one a new dress to the tailor's and the new plastic shoes to Katchawira's shop. True." This was some real gossip, and I enjoyed hearing it. It was one of the few things in the last year that Jordan had offered to me without my directly asking him, and it made me feel like an insider, a friend, and I enjoyed this, too.

"Well, that dumb bastard ought to keep his pecker in his pants. Then he'd have a little more money. Don't you think?"

Jordan looked at me with some obvious confusion. "What is this boss, the pecker? I do not know this word."

"His pecker, his *mbolo*. You know what I mean. He should keep his mbolo in his pants. Stop screwing ladies all the time."

Jordan appeared dumbfounded. He stared at me in a way that was new in our relationship. It was more than confusion, I knew, because he obviously understood me. It was more than embarrassment or shock. It was, it seemed, disgust. He would not look directly at me but preferred to gaze out the window and then down at the table. He became a little rigid. His body language indicated his uneasiness.

While I knew that all of us here used these Anglo-Saxon vulgarities frequently and that Jordan had often heard us, perhaps this was the first time he had been so directly confronted that he could not ignore it. "What's the matter?" I asked. "You didn't like my choice of words?"

Jordan hesitated. I had asked him a question, solicited his opinion and, given our relationship, was compelling him to answer.

"Oh, it is nothing, boss." He tried to let it drop.

"Come on. You didn't like what I said?" I pressed him. "I know it's a crazy expression, but it's just the way we talk. It doesn't mean anything. We just talk like that. You must have heard the azungus talk like that. Don't you have words like that in Chichewa?" I tried to lighten the situation and to bring him into it by claiming that all people spoke the same way.

Jordan waited a moment and without looking directly at me, he said, "No, boss. This is a no good word. The people cannot use words such as these." He paused again but went on, "I do not like. It is a no good thing to speak these words. Ah, no."

"Hell, it doesn't mean anything. It's practically a joke. Everyone says things like this," I protested, trying to justify my actions as being universal.

Jordan held his ground, "No, boss, this is a bad thing in which to say. We do not use words such as this. We do not like."

Jordan held to his position. He had passed judgment on me and the others—on all Europeans, actually—and he was maintaining his opinion. I tried a new tactic. "You mean to say that in the Chichewa language you don't swear? What happens when you get angry at someone? I've heard you yelling at people before. And what happens when you get drunk, like two weeks ago? Are you saying you don't swear?"

Jordan thought for a moment. "No, boss. I do not use words such as these."

I came back, "Now, Jordan, you admit you get angry at people, and you admit you get drunk, too. Don't you?"

"This is true. And I am a drinker, as you my boss know."

"But you don't swear? Is this what you're saying?"

"I do not use words such as my bosses."

"Oh, so you swear then. You just swear differently. I mean you don't use the same body parts like we do, like mbolo." I pressed on because I was enjoying our conversation and because I was learning something and because this was a slight reversal of our normal interaction. Generally, it was I who tried to understand his situation, to be tolerant, to place myself in his position. Now he was judging me and although it was over a minor issue in my opinion, I wanted to see how strongly he held to his position, to see how tenacious he would be in his judgment. "So you wouldn't call someone a dumb ass. You'd just say something like a dumb elbow. That it?" I suspected our conversation was not going to go much further, but I could not resist one more attempt at unraveling our differences. My comment was flip and probably unfair, for the entire mode of our swearing was obviously so different from Jordan's that there was no meaningful basis in comparison.

"Well no, boss. We cannot talk such as this." Jordan had come to the end. He did not like our expressions, it was clear. He found them vulgar and offensive. He also found references to body parts just plain stupid, incomprehensible. I wondered if these polite people simply used other types of colorful language. This seemed probable, and I knew I would just need to listen and observe more carefully in the year ahead.

I stood up and held out my hands, my palms facing him, my fingers pointed upward. "OK, fine. I understand." I thought it best to stop our little conversation, since it was going nowhere. I figured that in this social environment of eight other men all about my age I would continue to use my Anglo-Saxon profanity and that Jordan would simply have to live with it. I understood his position on the matter, and I found it interesting that while we now understood each other a little better, we did not come to any accommodation. It seemed we were both going to stick to our own way of doing things. This raised issues about cross-cultural understanding that I would need to sort out.

I turned and quickly went and got my shoes and socks, which were in the bedroom Mike and I shared, and brought them back to the kitchen table. As I sat down to put them on, I called to Jordan, who was now in the kitchen, "Say, achimwene, what's the story with the guys at the other house and Robert? Dixon and Bush said last night when they were here playing cards that they were going to get a new cook. They said that you were going to bring your cousin or your brother-in-law or something around to see them. Is this right?"

Jordan came to the kitchen door. "Yes, bwana. Today my good cousin, I should say my cousin-brother Lester, is coming. He is from near to my village."

"He's a real cook? Or is he just someone like Robert who can just do a little of this and that? I didn't think there were any real cooks in the district."

"Well, he is working to Bulaweyo to Rhodesia these so many years. He can be a real cook, my boss."

"How come he's back here in Ntcheu?"

"I do not know. But he has recently returned. He has been staying to Rhodesia, I should say, for perhaps eighteen years. He cooked for the madams and to the restaurants. He is a cook, I know."

"As good as you?" I asked to be playful.

"Oh no, boss. This cannot be," Jordan answered seriously.

"I hear he's better."

"You did, boss? Where is this you have heard this?"

"No, Jordan, I'm kidding. I don't even know this guy." I finished tying my shoes and stood up ready to go. "Say, you said he's your cousin-brother. What do you mean? Why isn't he your cousin or your brother?"

"Well, it is like that. It is a bit confusing for the Europeans. He can be my brother but he is not the brother, boss."

I thought a moment to clarify this little kinship riddle. "Let's see. This Lester is not the child of your parents. Correct?"

"Yes, boss," Jordan was paying careful attention.

"So we'd say he's not your brother. But he's the child of your father's brother. Right?"

"Ah, huh. This is it boss. So you know these things?"

"Well, just a little bit." I spoke like Jordan. "We'd say he's your cousin. But you say he's a special cousin, and you call him a brother. That it?" I felt silly trying to clarify Jordan's kinship system to him, but the Ngoni people, of which Jordan was a member, traced kinship through males, patrilineal descent; and many of the people with whom they lived in proximity, and with whom they sometimes married, were Chewas and Yaos, and these people were matrilineal and traced their descent through females. So in this area, two very different types of kinship systems had become mixed together, and one needed to be careful in analysis. Jordan's home now was in Ida's village; and this residence pattern at marriage, living with the wife's kinsmen, was the pattern not of the Ngonis, but of the original inhabitants of the region.

"You are so clever to these matters, my boss," Jordan praised me for something that was obviously commonplace to him. Perhaps he simply enjoyed the fact that I had tried to figure it out.

"But, Jordan, isn't this a little bit tricky? I mean how's poor Robert going to feel about it? He'll sort of be demoted, won't he?" I tried to read Jordan carefully, to see how he actually felt about Robert. For some time I had been confused over the Malawian cultural pattern, in which people were so polite, using honorific terms of address, and giving signs of *ulemu* or big respect to one another. It was an enjoyable social environment to live in because people constantly smiled at each other and shook hands and spoke gently to each other, and it probably functioned well in the small compact villages of Malawi where one's social interactions were not with strangers, but with kinsmen and well-known neighbors. The perplexing issue for me was to try to comprehend what was going on beneath the surface. Surely, all people did not get along. There must be plenty of disagreements and jealousies and animosities; and then too there were strangers, especially people like me, a privileged European, toward whom there was no good reason for being so friendly, other than to claim that this was the cultural pattern of the people. Jordan and Robert appeared to be good friends, and my impression was that they acted with the utmost respect for each other. I wondered why and whether this were really true. After all, Robert had been here before Jordan, and he had quickly been relegated to the lower rank of houseboy and then pushed out to a new household.

"Well, this is so, my boss," Jordan spoke softly. "But Robert can be the houseboy for the bwanas to that house and can work for my bwanas here on some of the days. So he cannot be sacked."

I could see that Jordan had given it some serious thought; and if Lester was hired, I was sure we would all go along with the new arrangement. I was not going to understand Jordan's real attitudes toward Robert at this time and as with so many subtle Malawian riddles, I was simply left to speculate about the dynamics of a society that placed such emphasis on the overt expression of politeness among its members.

"OK, then, Bambo Jordan. We'll work it out when we see what those guys are going to do." I smiled at Jordan, "I'm off. Ndapita. See you at lunch time. Oh, yes, I'll also make sure I see Misomali about Josephu."

"OK boss, pitani bwino," Jordan waved and gave me a big smile.

Chapter Six

Dancing in Place

"Odi," Mike called out as we stepped onto our neighbors' little khonde. We could see Bush sitting at the kitchen table writing a letter.

He looked up. "Hey, Mike, Bruce. Odini. Come in." He put his pen down and turned to us as we stepped into the living room of a house identical to ours. We set our soaked canvas bags containing our medical supplies and census forms onto the small sofa and shook the water from our arms. "You guys look great. Got caught in the rain, huh?"

"You're a brilliant bastard, Bushy," I quipped as I wiped my face.

"An astute observer of his physical world," Mike added to complete the razz. "What a pain out there today. We got nothing done, and we went out at one o'clock. Village work and the rainy season just don't make it."

"Where were you?" Bush asked seriously.

"We've been in Gumbu Village. A few miles on the other side of the secondary school. It's a pretty good hike." Mike added, "Right after lunch the rains stopped, so we left with Mbepula. Soon as we got to Gumbu, it really came down. All afternoon we stood under someone's khonde and got soaked and cold."

"We only read three Mantoux and worked with just one family. And only half of them were there. What a waste of time," I said. "Then it was the walk back in the rain, although it's lighter now."

Bush offered to make us coffee, and we quickly accepted. I was shivering slightly as we sat at the dining room table, and although I needed to get my wet clothes off, I always enjoyed stopping by to get the news of the day.

"Where's that deadbeat Dixon?" I called to Bush in the kitchen as he placed some wood into the stove.

He turned, smiled and said, "*Akugona* [He is sleeping]. What else? A stand-up member of the fifty-fifty club. Spends half his time asleep."

"Let's get the bastard up," Mike said with amusement. "He's supposed to be fighting ignorance, not sleeping his life away." He walked to the open door of Dixon's room and called him and insisted he come out and talk with us.

Bush and I could hear Dixon's groans, which he loudly affected for our benefit. Jokes about Dixon's sleeping habits were constantly going on among us, and we enjoyed any chance to add to them.

Soon the coffee was on the table, and Dixon came from his room, the effects of sleep still obvious on his face. Dixon was seven or eight years older than most of us and had taught in public high schools for a number of years in Seattle. He was the old man of the group, the experienced teacher, formal and more cautious in his behavior than any of the rest of us. He was neat in his appearance and in his habits. He was an astute observer of what went on around him and a superb storyteller, and he had the ability to see the humor in almost any situation, even difficult ones. As Dixon sat down at the table, the smiles on our faces indicated our anticipation of some type of silliness.

"I went in to read after school. Leaned back on the pillow and knocked myself out for four hours. And I only needed a little nap." This was Dixon's favorite line about his sleeping, and he always told it straight. We had all heard it so frequently that we just smiled. That was usually just enough encouragement for this funny man to go on and on.

"So the week's over, Bwana Dixon," I finally said. "All set for the big party tomorrow night?"

"God, no! Hell, it's going to be a nightmare. You guys are real beauties putting together something like this."

The three of us smiled. Our party was going to be a first for Ntcheu. Nothing like it was ever held in the seventy years of colonial control in the district. "What's the trouble? It should be fun," Mike replied.

"Come on. It's crazy. You've got every bum in the area coming," he insisted.

"What do you mean?" I answered. "We've got all the prominent people coming. Ian, all the teachers, the police chief, Misomali, and Tony are all coming. You can't get much more highfalutin than that. Hell, this is going to be a high-class affair."

Dixon shook his head and smiled. "Sure it is. A real black tie affair."

Dixon was ill-at-ease with what we had in mind, but I knew that his appreciation of the bizarre, the incongruous, would keep him interested as long as he could just stand off to the side and observe.

"Mike and I even got a band lined up," I bragged.

"What do you mean, a band? There's no band around here," Dixon replied.

"Sure there is," Mike explained. "You know that guy that plays the rusty old saxophone on some Saturday mornings in the market? Turns out he's got a band. A real Tommy Dorsey, that guy."

"Come on. You mean the guy in the hovel behind the market? The place with the hookers and all the drunks? He's got a band?" Dixon's cynicism was expected, but he was amused too.

"Sure does. It's a great band too," I answered. "There's a saxophone, with a few missing buttons, which highlights the band leader's virtuosity; a couple of drums, like bongo drums; a guy with a homemade guitar; and a kid with some stones that he puts into a couple of cans for maracas. Really, it's not bad."

"How did you organize this?" Dixon asked with increasing amusement.

"We were out in this new village the other day, and we met the saxophone player. We asked him if he'd like to play with his full band," Mike explained.

"How much you going to give him?" Dixon asked.

"Five pounds," I said.

"Five pounds. You're crazy. That guy's never seen five pounds in his life."

"True," I replied. "We screwed up. We lost our minds. I guess we were so happy to find him. He's got a busy schedule."

"Shit, you could have hired him for one pound. Hell, the Ntcheu symphony plays for five pounds."

"You're right. Anyway, that's the deal and we've got to live with it."

Dixon was thoroughly amused. "Bushy says you even invited the raggedy woodman. That true?"

Bush laughed and Mike smiled. "Sure, why not? He comes around every once in a while with our wood. He's part of things," I answered.

"Hell, the guy doesn't have any clothes," Dixon stated. "This guy is really from the village. People from the hospital staff I understand, but this guy's right out of the bush. He doesn't speak a word of English, does he? What are guys like Ian and Misomali going to say?"

"That's their problem," Mike answered. "Jordan and Robert and Lester and the new guy, Paxton, are coming too. The more the merrier."

"How did the raggedy woodman hear about it?"

"I don't know," Bush answered. "He came yesterday with a big load of wood. I was bargaining with him through Lester, and he asked Lester if he could come to the big party."

"How did he hear about it?" Dixon was loving this.

"I guess he heard about it in the village," Bush replied.

"In the village! God, there'll be a hundred freeloaders beating at the doors." Dixon's amusement waned a bit.

"Well, he's so strong, we'll make him the bouncer," I continued, "Besides, people won't crash the party, really."

"So what are you going to serve at this grand affair, champagne?"

Mike outlined the menu. "Beer, wine, Cokes and Fanta. And we've got some popcorn and roasted groundnuts, and Jordan's going to make a few loaves of bread, and we'll serve slices with peanut butter. It's going to be first class. And Jordan's going to make a cake if he gets time."

"How much booze you going to have?"

Bush and Devendorff, the third roommate in their house, were handling the alcohol. Bush explained, "We've got six cases of beer now. And Ian drove John up to Bili Wili and on through to Mozambique to pay one of the Portuguese bar owners to bring down a twenty-five-gallon barrel of wine. Some guy we met last week at Dias's bar up there. And we've got four gallons already. That should be enough."

"Thirty gallons of rotgut." Dixon was incredulous. "How many do you expect, anyway?"

"About thirty, maybe even fifty. Hey, we do things right. Got to keep the bwana image up," Bush replied with a big grin. "Why skimp now? You think Emily Post would run out of wine at her party?" Mike laughed, and Dixon lowered his forehead into his hands.

"And what about the young lovelies? How many little *atzikana* [girls] are coming?" Dixon smiled. He wanted to understand the complete guest list.

"Who knows? As many as show up. Mike and I asked a few female health assistants at the hospital. But mostly we just spread the word to the guys we asked. Don't worry, they'll all bring lady friends." While I was afraid that we might not have done a good job of inviting women, many people lived within a quarter of a mile of our home, and the guest list could be expanded at the last minute.

Bush spoke to the issue. "Young Bob and I asked the good ladies at Manda's to come too."

Dixon chuckled then said, "Come on. That's too much. You can't mix these broads in with these civil servants. It's just not going to fly."

"Screw 'em. These ladies are some of our best friends. The big wigs will just have to live with it. We're not prejudiced against working girls." Bush's answer was unsatisfactory to Dixon, but this was to be a freewheeling event, and none of us were willing to exclude anyone we had dealings with. He continued, "And Dix, we made a special request that the little beauty Lucy come. The one with the nice boobs."

"Lucy. She's coming? Really?" Dixon smiled and his eyes twinkled a bit. He infrequently went to Manda's because he did not like being constantly harassed by the clientele to buy them beer. However, he liked the setting and the social dynamics of the little bar. While it was really just a fancy hut, having iron sheets on the roof, a real concrete floor, and three small tables and a handful of chairs, it had a paraffin refrigerator and was one of the few places where you could get a cold drink. Of special interest to us all were the two good tilly lanterns which kept the place well lit and made it the brightest among all the shops at Mphate. The bar girls were from the neighboring villages, and they came to Manda's, it seemed, to get free beer as much as to be with men. They were a far cry from the flashy prostitutes of Blantyre who spoke English and wore decent clothing. In rural areas like this, where people resided in villages and the girls were tied closely to their families, sexual behavior, especially that of their daughters, was quite strictly regulated. That a double standard was operating, with all the conflicts this implied, was obvious, however. Men could chase women without much negative sentiment, but young women were to remain close to home.

Our conversation continued as we went over the details. We would combine every glass and teacup from the two households, and people would have to share if too many showed up. We would get ten pounds of sugar for those who liked to mix it into the wine for what was considered an enhancement to the wine's effect. We would borrow lanterns and some records for our battery-powered player. It was set. The party was organized.

Our male guests began arriving as soon as it got dark, more than an hour early. Jordan and Paxton, who was now our part-time houseboy, were still washing the dinner dishes and Bastone and I had yet to change into our party clothes. Mike simply acted as the good host and put on some records and began passing out warm beers and glasses of the cheap red wine. Fortunately, the guests were from the hospital staff, and they seemed comfortable chatting with each other. Things changed quickly. Within an hour the house was filled, and the party was in full swing. The wine and beer were going very fast, and the guests were dancing. Ntcheu's elites filtered in shortly, and many of these men had girls from the secondary school with them; their wives who lived close-by were left at home. Bush, Devendorff, and Bob, along with Lester and Robert, joined all of us, and the wine began to flow even faster.

Our rag tag band finally arrived. Not one musician had shoes, but they had their instruments, and this excited the guests. As we moved the dining room table against a wall to give them space to play, the band members, including the young boy who played the tin cans, quickly availed themselves of the free wine.

Mike and Dan had stationed themselves near the huge wine barrel and had taken it upon themselves to serve. It was a difficult task since the guests generally drank it as fast as their glasses were filled and were constantly forming little lines. Some, like people doing shots, simply threw their heads back and gulped it, and no one seemed concerned with its effects. The band members, having arrived late, seemed determined to get their share and before they attempted to play had consumed considerable quantities.

As hosts, we were not immune from the effects of all this liquor either. While we generally drank with a little more restraint, as did our educated Malawian friends, it was clear that all of us were beginning to feel tipsy.

The band was now playing, and our records were put away. The guests loved *kwela* music, which was found throughout this area of east-central Africa. Our little makeshift band, while having its own version of this popular African music, had the talent to bring out the strong repeating rhythms that were so easy to dance to. Our problem was that the band was much more interested in the wine and beer than in making music, and our guests were becoming annoyed with their frequent breaks to drink. Nevertheless, the party moved on without major problems, and our friends seemed to be having a grand time.

Dixon arrived an hour or so late. His curiosity would never allow him to miss a scene so complex—one with potential storytelling material that could last him for weeks. He simply stood in the space between the dining room and living room by the refrigerator with a small glass of wine and smoked cigarettes. He did not talk much; he was there to observe and to stay above it all.

The living room was full of dancers now, twisting and jitterbugging, sweating and drinking, and we were right in the middle of it. It was difficult to rest; for as soon as a person stopped moving, there would be an invitation to dance some more. On and on we went. The saxophone, its rhythms compelling, beckoned us to move, to dance. The booze, its powers so obvious, removed the remaining inhibitions from even the most uptight among us. There was no excuse to refrain. It was truly a party, a brief hour or two for forgetting all the troubles of this difficult place and being happy, a time to live life a little more completely. I had never experienced an event like this that seemed to bring so much pleasure; it seemed right and good to me. It brought joy to a few people, however briefly, and they, resigned to a difficult daily struggle to survive, deserved some moments like this.

The band continued to take constant breaks so that the members could gulp down more beer and wine, and it was during these times that we and our guests would scatter into the nearby gardens to urinate. To see men urinating at the side of a road was a familiar scene in all the Third World, and we had all been on bus trips in which the driver would simply stop and direct men to the bushes on one side and women to the other. This night our yard was full of children and teenagers from the boma who had come to observe the adults' big party and to listen through the open windows to the music, and this crowd made our private acts into somewhat public affairs. Perhaps it was all the alcohol we had consumed, but it did not seem to bother anyone, and it seemed consistent with the rest of our uninhibited actions.

Jordan had occasionally brought bread and peanuts to the tables, but he and his helpers had little else to do except to enjoy themselves. Jordan and Lester, it appeared, mixed in easily with most of the guests in spite of the clear difference in status between a cook and a civil servant. Both Robert and Paxton, who were very much simple villagers, just stood off to the side and watched, although it seemed they did it with enthusiasm.

As the band members took yet another beer break, someone had placed a Johnny Mathis record on the player. The guests preferred the faster moving kwela music, and so most stepped from the center of the room to give space to the few ballroom dancers. As I sat on our little couch and wiped the perspiration from my forehead, Jordan sat down beside me.

"Having fun, Jordan?" I asked.

"Oh, boss, this is a very wonderful party. For my whole life I have not had a time as this. It is too very good," Jordan spoke seriously.

"You think the people are having fun?"

"Oh, yes, boss. This I know. The people have spoken to me. They cannot know such a night before." The alcohol having loosened his tongue, he continued, "These people cannot have a party such as this to the villages. For the puberty, there is the party. We can have the chicken and goat meat and the *mowa* [traditional beer] for the drinking and there is the dancing. And to the weddings, there is the party to the celebrations. But not such as this. No."

Jordan hesitated a moment and looked up at the sweaty dancers.

He finally turned and surprisingly spoke again, "But the celebrations to the village can still be good." He looked directly at me, "Are you hearing, my boss?"

I smiled and answered. "I think I hear you. You're saying that parties at home in the village don't have as much food or beer or fancy music, but they're still nice affairs and that a good time does not depend on the money to buy things. People make a party fun. Right?"

"This can be, boss. But it is a bit more." Again he thought for a moment. "The beer and the food such as we are having the people cannot know. But to the village, it is a bit more as I have said. It is the celebration of the things of the life. Such as to the wedding. We can have the party and the fun but we can also have the celebration. So it is more."

I looked at Jordan trying to understand him. Finally I spoke, "I think I've got it now, achimwene. These celebrations would be very special parties. Important days that we can always remember. When special things happen. But what of regular parties like this? Just to have fun."

"No, boss. We village people can have no money. Some can drink if having the *kwacha* [Money; Unit of currency] but there is no big party."

"Well, what celebration do you remember best?"

"The best celebration, boss?"

"Yes, your favorite event. Was it your wedding?"

"My wedding to my Ida, boss? I do not think. You see we just got married and told the people. So it was easy."

"No ceremony?"

"No, boss."

"Well, what then? You said they were better than parties," I pressed him.

Jordan thought for a few moments. He spoke softly. "It was the funeral to the mother of your Jordan. All the people came and there was much food to eat. It was a very big respect the people gave."

"But wasn't it a sad day?"

"Yes, boss. But there was big respect and much food and the people could chat to each other. And the mother can die and go to be with the God. So it is good too."

"That's nice, Jordan. And interesting too. But have you been to a party like this one before?"

"Me, boss? I can know of parties because I am a houseboy and cook to the big bwanas to Blantyre and Rhodesia. So I know. But these people, no it cannot be."

"So you've been around," I said.

"Well, yes. Well, I know these civil servants are superior to me.

They can have the education and the jobs which I do not have. But still they cannot know of a party such as this. And these village people are too amazed. Never can they imagine."

"There's only five or six guys from the village, wouldn't you say? The woodman and some guy he brought and the guy over there who is a carpenter near Eneya Village. And those three others who hang around the market, or maybe they work for the Indians at the shops," I said.

"This seems to be true."

"They all seem to be having fun. I think they're all very drunk too, especially the woodman's friend."

"Oh, boss, they are very drunk indeed. Too bloody drunk. It is no good," Jordan spoke, his own voice slurred.

"You don't think we should have invited them, then?"

"No, boss, this is a no good place for the people such as these. No."

"Why not?"

"Because they are just these little people from the village. What do people such as these know? They cannot be with the bwanas such as Mkandwire and Misomali and the big teachers such as Ngoma and Pachameya."

"You snobby bastard, Jordan. I can't believe you. Aren't they regular people just like you? I mean they have probably never had a chance to go to much school, like you. So they're the same as you. Actually, we're all the same, just people. Some of us have had more chances, that's all."

"No, boss. These people can be different," Jordan insisted.

"Different? How? Don't you live in the village from time to time? Aren't you a villager really?"

"This is true but I can be different. I am not the same as these people. I am a clever chap. I am a cook, the best cook, and I am handsome too," he boasted.

"Yeah, you're a clever, handsome cook, all right," I spoke quickly. "But does this make you any better than these men?"

Jordan thought for a moment, then turned and looked at me. His eyes were unfocused from all the wine, and he simply said, "This is how the things are."

I was uneasy with Jordan's comments. He was a proud man, intelligent and capable, and had more going for himself than most people. I was determined to follow up on this conversation later, but I knew I was not going to get far under these conditions. Jordan had partially outlined his view of the status hierarchy, moral assessment and all, and where he placed himself in it; he was above the peasant since he had skills and worked for wages. My Malawian friends here were certainly no less immune from ranking people than Americans were, but if my impressions were correct, their classifications were even stricter and more important to them. I wondered how Jordan felt about those above him in the scheme and why he was so adamant in claiming superiority over the village men.

"Say, achimwene, let's get some more wine before it's gone." I tapped Jordan on the leg as I stood to indicate that he should join me at the wine barrel. Jordan stood and followed me to where Bastone was standing with John. The two had now assumed the bartender roles and were ladling out the wine from the top of the barrel with a pot from the kitchen.

"You see who's dancing?" John grinned and nodded toward the dance floor. I turned to see Dixon in the embrace of Mr. Makwangwala, the leader of the district branch of the Malawi Congress Party. He was a huge man, close to three hundred pounds, I guessed, and his great bulk made Dixon appear like a small boy. Makwangwala was one of our favorite friends in the boma because he was pleasant and bright and because he had helped us on a number of projects. At the moment, he was having some local men build a tuberculosis ward at the hospital, a major undertaking for this poor district, since the funds were all raised locally.

It was a terrific sight—Johnny Mathis crooning a love song and Makwangwala steering old Dixon around the dance floor. Like two young children at their first dance class, stiff and awkward, they moved with labored steps around and around. Makwangwala seemed pleased. His forehead glistened with sweat and his great stomach stuck out from his brown suit coat that he could no longer button, but he was smiling and appeared to be thoroughly enjoying himself. Dixon, however, was obviously uncomfortable, and when his eyes would catch ours, they asked for understanding. We had all been in a similar predicament here in Malawi and had danced with men before, and we knew how basically innocent and friendly a gesture it was to dance like this. Intellectually, we knew it was simply our culture that defined it as unacceptable, but this made it only slightly less difficult to accept when put in the situation. The fact that Dixon, who had planned not to participate in our party, was now more involved than any of us was a special treat. Bastone and John and I fought not to giggle but our subdued smiles and our nods of approval to Makwangwala as he danced by let Dixon know we were enjoying the moment immensely.

"Why don't you dance, Jordan?" Bastone asked.

"Me, sir?"

"You haven't danced yet, have you?" Bastone continued.

"No, sir. But who should I dance with?" Jordan asked.

"Anyone. Just ask someone."

Jordan thought carefully. "Well, would you dance with me?" He addressed Bastone, who had encouraged him.

"Ah, Jordan. I don't like to dance, really. Why don't you ask one of the girls? It's better that way." Bastone was polite and gentle in his refusal, but because Jordan was his employee, it was easy for him to turn down the request. I suspected he would have danced if anyone else had asked him.

Jordan said nothing but simply turned and looked out at the dancers. I did not blame Bastone, for he meant no harm. It is likely that I would have done the same, but it certainly underscored the issue of status in our little ranked society. While the exchange was quick and we passed it off, it must have pained Jordan, even on this night of fun.

We stood for several minutes watching the dancers and sipping wine. I could see Jordan glancing at a pretty secondary-school girl of perhaps seventeen who was standing near us in another small group of onlookers. He set his glass down and stepped toward her. He reached his hand out and took hers, and in one motion he asked her to dance and then gently pulled her to the dance area. She reacted quickly and pulled her hand from Jordan and stepped back and continued to look past Jordan to the dancers.

Jordan spoke up quickly in English, "What, you do not wish to dance with me?" His eyes were focused and stern, his voice loud and demanding a reply.

The young girl said nothing.

"I say, will you not dance with me, girl?" Jordan's voice became louder.

She did nothing but continued to stare past him.

Jordan stepped in front of her. "Girl, I am speaking to you. Do you wish to dance with me? Do you hear me, girl?" Jordan's voice was even louder, and he spoke more firmly.

The young girl would not acknowledge him and continued to stare beyond him.

Now Jordan was angry, and as the group of us looked over to him, he began to shout, "I, Jordan, am asking you to dance. What do you say, girl?"

She hesitated and Jordan waited. At last she spoke. "No, I will not dance." She replied firmly without looking at him.

"What? You cannot dance with me?" Jordan was infuriated, and perhaps embarrassed too, since his loud voice was now beginning to attract attention. He continued, "I, Jordan, am asking you this time to dance. You cannot refuse. I am a big man. What do you say? Come."

She stepped behind one of the young men from the hospital and said again, this time with a quick glance in his direction, "No, I will not."

"You are a bitch girl, a bad bitch girl. This cannot be. You are a child and you cannot refuse a big man such as me!" Jordan was pointing and shouting at her, and nearly everyone in the room was now watching the painful scene.

To try to end it, I stepped forward, behind Jordan, and put my entire right arm over his right shoulder and across his chest and gently hugged him to me. I spoke into his left ear and asked him to forget the dance and suggested in a soft voice that we drink some more wine. I gently turned him around and directed him back to the wine barrel and Mike and Bastone. He spun from my grip as he became more angry and embarrassed and screamed back to the young woman, "You are a fuck girl, a fuck girl. You cannot do this!"

This time I moved quickly and grabbed his shoulders from behind. The giant Makwangwala stepped between Jordan and the girl and simply looked down at him. This man of great authority and prestige in the community had acted without speaking, but he left no doubt that the messy scene was to stop. I turned Jordan around firmly and walked him back again to the wine barrel.

To ease the tension and to help deflect the stares which were all on Jordan, Mike spoke out quickly to the saxophonist, who was across the room, and asked him to assemble the band for more music. This focused the attention on a new subject, and there were smiles and chuckles in the room as our chief musician mumbled a few very drunken words in Chichewa. Mike was confused, and finally Mbepula, our counterpart on the tuberculosis project, explained, with a good deal of amusement in his voice, that the band was completely drunk and incapable of going on. The drummer, he explained, had passed out in the dirt driveway in the front of the house, and the young boy was last seen vomiting, but no one knew where he was. To our relief, the guests took an interest in this bad news and, after a little conversation among themselves, most followed the lead of two men who began to shout at the band leader, insisting that drunk or not, the band had to play.

Jordan remained upset. He was clearly embarrassed and he was still angry. Bastone and I tried to comfort him and also tried to get him to calm down.

"Come on, achimwene. Let's go outside and see the drunk drummer." I grabbed his hand, and we walked slowly behind the guests and out to the driveway, where we stopped and stood for a moment.

"Oh, boss. I do not understand. This girl she is just a schoolgirl and I am a big man, a grown man. I am having a family. She must give me the respect. But no she does not. It is no good. She is a bad one." Jordan outlined his feelings, and I felt sorry for him. Perhaps the girl was shy, and a party like this would be an even newer experience for her than for others, but I suspected as Jordan implied that she simply felt too good for Jordan. He was only a cook, after all. She was one of Malawi's privileged citizens, one of a tiny number who ever got to secondary school, one of the future elites.

"Forget it, Jordan," I said. "Hell, these things happen all the time. It could have happened to any one of us, especially since we're all drunk."

He thought for a moment. "Yes, boss. This is perhaps true and we are very drunk indeed. But I do not like this one."

I touched his face, "Come on, man. Let's not talk about it now. Tomorrow maybe. OK?"

Jordan spoke softly, "OK, boss, tomorrow."

"Good. Now let's go and finish the booze and get good and drunk. You take a little walk first, and I'll see if I can get the band going again."

Jordan agreed, and he turned and began to walk slowly up our drive toward the boma. As I returned to the house, I felt very sorry that this proud man had to go through such an episode. But I knew that once he was outside the village, nearly everyone would have a higher social position than he and that many, especially the recently advanced, would not hesitate to display it.

My good friend Ian, now the district commissioner, whom I saw almost daily, passed me as I entered the front door.

"Boy, I'm sorry this little incident happened, Ian. It's really too bad, you know."

"Yes, it is. But when you start mixing people like this with these uneducated chaps, it just doesn't work. And these secondary-school kids know they are very special. Cooks are nothing to them." Ian spoke not to scold, only to inform, but I did not enjoy hearing him.

"I guess so," I answered and kept moving.

As I stepped into the living room again, I noticed a group of four men engaged in an animated conversation with the band leader and the guitar player. I walked quickly to the dining area and stood with Bush and Dan behind the group as they took turns berating the pair for their inability to go on playing. The poor leader, his saxophone lying on the dining room table beside him, was so drunk now that he could do little but stand with his partner, their eyes turned to the floor, and take the abuse. The men insisted that drunkeness was no excuse and that the band play. The people wanted to dance, and the players must fulfill their obligations. The four took turns explaining themselves, and their voices became louder and more aggressive.

The drummer staggered through the kitchen door toward us, followed by two men who, I assumed, had retrieved him from his brief sleep in the driveway. He stood for a moment and stared at us as if trying to comprehend what was happening, or perhaps even where he was. His face was without expression, but his eyes were heavy, and he fought to keep them open. His bottom lip drooped forward. He was a sorry sight, but I did not have to look at him for very long because he was incapable of standing. In seconds, he stepped back against the wall, and once there he slowly slid down, sat for a few seconds, then slumped to his left, his head resting on the floor.

I started to laugh, but the four antagonists began to complain even more loudly that the leader should keep his men in line, which kept the ridiculous scene as serious as ever. One stepped to the drummer and gently kicked him to see if there was a possibility of reviving him.

Without speaking, the leader reached for his saxophone and gestured for the drunken guitarist to get his instrument. The young boy was still missing, and the drummer had passed out on the floor, but these two, reluctantly, were going to play—half a band was better than none.

Bush and Dan and I quietly walked away. We agreed that it was severe treatment to force the musicians to go on but decided to let the incident play out by itself without our interference. It did not seem to matter now. The wine was about finished, the beer and soft drinks and the food were gone and most all the guests, with the exception of the young women, appeared to be very drunk. The dancing had nearly stopped too, and many of the party-goers began to circulate through the room to shake hands and to offer their thanks. The band tried once again, but the leader himself was no longer capable of making his instrument work, and after a few false starts the guitarist had joined his friend the drummer on the floor. The party was winding down, death from unnatural causes, and the guests began filtering out into the night.

Jordan joined me at the wine barrel, and we split the last little bit of wine, and Mike turned off the record player for the last time to signal the end of the evening. I simply stood and shook hands with the remaining guests as they politely made their round of farewells. I said little to them, and they just smiled or even laughed outright to express their gratitude. I knew they had had fun, and I was pleased.

Within minutes the guests were gone. Even our two sleeping musicians had mysteriously disappeared, although I suspected with considerable help. Jordan and I sat on the little couch, and the others found chairs and joined around us. Story after story was told, and it was agreed that the evening was a great success. Cleanup would take place in the morning; Dan and Bastone and Dixon decided to turn in for the night while the rest of us would walk the two miles up to Manda's Bar to find Lucy and the other girls who had stood us up.

I informed the gang that I would catch up with them at the bar. I wished to talk to Jordan, and they seemed to understand.

"Jordan, let me steer you home. I think you need a driver."

"Oh, I can make it, my bwana."

"Come on, I'll walk with you." We got up, and I grabbed a lantern and started out through the kitchen toward the servant's quarters in the back when we noticed the young maraca player curled up asleep on the floor of a little storage closet. We decided to leave him there for the night, or until he woke, since his village was probably far away, and this was as good a place as any to sleep it off.

We shut the kitchen door but did not lock it, so that the boy could get out when he wished. We stepped into the space between the house and Jordan's quarters and stopped to talk.

"Say, Jordan, that was funny Makwangwala dancing with Dixon, wasn't it?"

"It was very nice, my boss," Jordan responded seriously. He then went on, "I take Makwangwala to be a good man. He was to South Africa as a boxer and for some time when he returned he had such a big fishing boat to the lake shore. He was too rich, boss."

"I didn't know that," I answered. "What happened to his business?"

"Well, boss, during these colonial times, I should say the emergency times, he is selling the business and giving the money to the party for the independence. This I know can be true."

"So he gave all his money away, and he's broke now. That's quite a story," I said.

"Well, he is a too big man now because the prime minister has made him to be the boss to the party here to Ntcheu. So he is the big man to the people," Jordan explained.

"That's a nice story, achimwene. It makes me like him even more." I could see Jordan's eyes were beginning to close even as we stood making small talk. The wine had finally gotten to him. "Jordan, I think it's time to sleep. Come on, I'll walk you to the quarters." I put my arm around his shoulders, and we shuffled the last twenty yards to his room.

We stopped at the door. Inside Ida and three of the children were asleep. "You OK, my good friend? It was a good party, wasn't it? People seemed to have a good time," I spoke up.

"It was a wonderful party, boss. The people had a too good time. Very wonderful," Jordan spoke quietly, without energy or enthusiasm.

"I'm sorry about the dance, Jordan. A silly young girl who thinks she's special. Don't worry about it, OK? It's no big deal."

Jordan searched for words. He reached out and held both my arms near my shoulders, and I reached out and held him near his elbows. He spoke more softly, "I am too sorry for this to happen." We held each other for a few moments, and then Jordan turned, opened the door, and stepped into the little room.

Chapter Seven

A Question of Style

John Devendorff and I joined Doug Smith, a new science teacher at the secondary school, for a Saturday morning stroll to the Ntcheu market. Our weekends seemed to pass slowly since the teachers were off, and Mike and I usually just stopped by the hospital for an hour or so. Finding things to occupy our time was a challenge for all of us Peace Corps volunteers, and the chance to spend a few hours in the shops at Mphate and at the large open market offered some excitement, since there were lots of people milling around buying food and socializing.

The market appeared less crowded than the usual Saturday. Not many vegetables were in season, and the offerings were limited. Nonetheless, it was a colorful sight. The women sellers, who had hauled their goods for many miles, wore their brightest and prettiest dresses; and the buyers, often with their entire families, milled throughout the market to examine the produce, to bargain intently, and to spend their pennies. Market day was an important event in this little agricultural community. It provided needed income for the growers and offered all a chance to leave the narrow social environment of their villages, to meet old friends, to gossip, and to get the news. It was a festive scene, and while the transactions were serious business, the people always appeared animated and full of energy.

We walked slowly through the market and stopped to examine the large clay pots that the women made locally and the strong woven baskets that were the handicrafts of the men. Because there were no tourists in this remote area, there were no curios or wooden carvings produced locally. But this day a young man had two simple

77

guitars for sale, goatskins serving as the sounding boards. Ntcheu was a relatively cool, high-altitude area of the country and was a big potato-growing region, and these were in abundance this day. The Ngoni people are a cattle-owning people, and beef is generally available, along with goats and an occasional pig. This day a bull had been slaughtered. Chickens, their legs tied with strands of grass, were stored in little baskets on the ground and were sold alive.

We spotted Jordan and Lester at the back edge of the market, where the butchering took place, and we made our way toward them. Our two cooks did all our buying. We simply gave them money on the two market days each week, and they left early in the morning to get what they thought was appropriate. It was an honor system, and we did not ask for any accounting of the money. The system was good for all of us, since none of the volunteers needed to go with them, and the cooks clearly enjoyed this aspect of their job. It afforded them a position of considerable importance and prestige in the market because they controlled an expenditure, some ten pounds each week, far in excess of the amounts spent by anyone else in the area. The fact that they might not bargain as diligently with our money as with their own was of little consequence since the sums were so small and because none of us could do as well if we had negotiated.

As we passed the covered brick counter where the meat was sold, Jordan and Lester spotted us and waved for us to come over to them. They were a sight to behold. Like aspiring movie actors resplendent in their finest outfits and hopeful that the world would see and appreciate them, they posed like peacocks. Dressed in white shirts, nice ties, neatly pressed pants, and shiny black shoes with socks, they seemed to have it all. Lester especially sparkled in the sunshine since he had worn his gold waiter's jacket, which he had obtained from some job long ago. To complete their effect, they wore sunglasses and held bicycles that we had lent them. They were handsome, successful, and to be envied.

"How are you two swingers doing?" John asked as we approached them.

They smiled and Lester laughed. "We are just fine, my bosses," Jordan answered.

"You're a couple of real dandies. All the women must be in love with you two," I said.

"Dandies, boss?" Jordan questioned.

"Fancy gentlemen. You know." I provided a definition.

"Oh, this is so, boss. The women can find us to be very handsome." Jordan and Lester smiled and stood a little straighter, as if to confirm the truth of the observation.

"Are you done shopping?" John asked.

"We are waiting to the butcher to get the good meat. We will buy the pork for the roast. Our baskets are too full now and so we have placed them to our friend, the tailor, to the Indian Shop just there." Jordan pointed to a store outside the market area. "We are just chatting with the friends to this time."

"If you guys want to meet us up at Dasu's store in a few minutes, you're welcome. We'll get a Coke or something. Then we'll help you carry the stuff home," John said.

They agreed, and the three of us continued our stroll through the market. Then, as we were about to pass through the gate that led back to the road, Doug stopped and said he wanted to ask Lester something. He would meet us at Dasu's.

John and I walked the quarter-mile past a half-dozen shops which lined each side of the road until we came to Dasu's. We each wanted to cash a check, and since Ntcheu did not have a bank, the two Dasu brothers served as our bankers. In return for this convenience, we generally made all our purchases at their shop.

The Dasus were quite sophisticated men in their thirties. Each had gone to secondary school in England, and they appeared clever to me and were always friendly, if also somehow a little distant. I had talked to them many times and had on one occasion traveled with them by lorry to Blantyre when they purchased supplies. Like many in the Indian community, they were born in Malawi and had visited India only briefly. Their grandparents had immigrated to the former colony years ago, probably not long after the turn of the century, and had quickly become merchants and traders. Many Asians in Malawi had become well-to-do, owning large companies for importing, transporting, and distributing goods, and the Dasus were the largest retail merchants in our district.

Indian shops were scattered throughout the country, and one could find shops hours away from the main roads in areas of extreme isolation. The Indian shopkeepers were obviously shrewd and competent businessmen; and while they performed an important role in the economy, the Malawians generally disliked and distrusted them. These were the merchants who actually took the money that one had worked so hard to earn, and because they posted no prices in their shops, they bargained—and they bargained hard—with each poor customer. The local people could not travel far to compare prices but were captives of the shopkeepers of an area, and it appeared that the Indians colluded to keep prices high. The fact that there were never sales or special discounts reinforced this impression. Colonialism had worked remarkably well in this regard. The British ran the big farms and big businesses, and the homeland pocketed the profits; the Indians earned the hatred of the people.

The Dasus' shop was large, perhaps sixty feet long. They had five full-time tailors who sat on the covered khonde which stretched the length of the building. Two sets of double doors opened into the shop and provided the only lighting. The shop was stuffed with goods—hardwares, bolts of bright cloth reaching to the ceiling, sacks of wheat flour—any item for which there was a market. The Dasus had the Coke distributorship in the district, and so cases of Coke and Fanta were stacked throughout. Importantly for us, they had a paraffin refrigerator from which we could purchase cold drinks.

The shop was crowded, and the two Dasus, one of their wives and a sister, and one Malawian man were working behind the giant counter that stretched along the entire length of the back wall. This was a busy day, and no sales were to be missed. John and I stood quietly behind two old women who were about to purchase some cloth when the older Dasu came over to greet us and asked what we would like. John explained that we wished to cash checks and would like two Cokes. Dasu shouted to a teenage boy who was working the floor area of the shop to get us the Cokes, and we stepped forward and wrote out the checks and got our money. We then went outside and sat on the khonde steps to watch the people as they walked from the market.

Doug soon arrived and joined us on the steps. He explained that he had asked Lester to purchase the bladder of one of the large animals that had been slaughtered. He planned an osmosis experiment in his biology class on Monday, and he would use the bladder as the membrane through which to pass the sugar. John and I listened with little interest. It seemed like a reasonable idea, but we said nothing. The three of us simply continued to watch the busy people.

Within twenty minutes, Jordan and Lester arrived with the food baskets strapped to the carriers of the bicycles. Doug went inside and bought two more Cokes for them, and they sat down to relax and join in the people watching.

"Did you guys get everything?" John asked.

"Yes, sir," Lester answered. Generally, he let Jordan do the talking.

"Did you get the bladder, Lester?" Doug asked.

His face began to flush. Clearly, he was embarrassed. "Yes, I have bought it." He glanced at Jordan for support, and suddenly the two of them burst into laughter. Then quickly they stopped and tried to restore their amused faces to normal. It was hopeless, and they burst into even more hearty laughter, the type that overwhelms. Lester shut his eyes tightly and kept his body rigid. Only his shoulders jumped up and down, as he tried to restrain himself and to reduce the possibility of offense. His laughter was without sound, but his shaking body gave him away. Jordan fought valiantly to maintain control too, but the task proved most difficult. He burst from the step, running away from the four of us. He bent forward at the waist as he moved, his arms crossed over his chest, his laughter projected forward so that the passers-by began to stare in our direction.

The three of us began to laugh too, with caution and uncertainty, conceding to them the moment, but not knowing why. "What's so funny, you guys?" Doug finally asked. "Come on, tell us."

When they had gained control of themselves, Jordan came and stood before the four of us, who were still seated. He began to speak in English. Then glancing at Lester, he mumbled just enough words in Chichewa to make them start again, and off they went through their entire laughing routine, while we, not wanting to be left out, chuckled along like fools, again not knowing why.

A group of perhaps ten had gathered around us on the steps of the khonde by the time Jordan and Lester had gained full control. We all waited for an explanation. Jordan went to his bicycle, grabbed a large package wrapped in newspaper, and set it on the top step. Then he began.

"You see, my bosses, the Bwana Smith here explained to the good Lester here to purchase for him this thing. I do not know what it is to English. Well, it is you know, my bosses, the place where the urine can be to the animal. What is this?"

"A bladder. It's called a bladder. A urinary bladder," Doug spoke up.

"Yes. The bladder. I know this now." Jordan continued, "Well, my Lester, he does not know this word. It is just a bit confusing, you see. Well, when he explains to the butcher, this is the trouble, the confusion." Jordan glanced at Lester and stopped to gain more control of himself. "Well, the butcher does not know and Lester is a bit too confused. And so the butcher has just given the entire thing." He unwrapped the newspaper slowly and with great drama. There it was, the bladder, the entire penis, and the testicles. Jordan screamed out, "It is this bladder thing but it can be the mbolo as well!"

Jordan stepped back, his ten fingers pointing down at the package as if he were making an offering. We leaned forward to see better, and the onlookers leaned over our shoulders for their glance.

Jordan's voice strained, rose in pitch, and began to be mixed with laughter. "The people to the market wish to know the type of food my bwanas prefer. And, to know what type of cooks are Lester and Jordan who can be cooking the bwanas such food as this. Is this azungu food they can ask? Oh, it is too funny. The people they are just laughing. They cannot believe. Ah, it is too funny. The whole mbolo thing. Ah, it cannot be."

While the three of us laughed hard, we were just a bit restrained, because the joke was on us. As we laughed, Jordan now explained with exaggerated arm movements and great drama in his voice to the crowd what he had just told us. As he finished, the crowd was howling in laughter too. Several people clapped their hands or pointed at the object of such amusement, and two teenage boys sprinted down the khonde to explain at the top of their voices Jordan's story to the tailors.

Several men who were strolling by came to inspect the package upon hearing the laughter and commotion. At first they just looked, but as the story was explained, and they learned that the people at the market thought this was the food of the azungu, they would soon be laughing too.

Jordan and Lester were center stage and appeared to be enjoying this immensely. The story was told over and over as new people came to see and listen. John, Doug, and I were incapable of understanding the rapid and colloquial Chichewa; but it appeared the story was becoming more elaborate, more embellished, each time it was told. It was a nice scene, enjoyed by storytellers and listeners alike, and it was good to see the humor of the situation so thoroughly enjoyed.

When things finally calmed down, we readied ourselves to leave. Jordan went ahead to buy a large can of milk powder, and we returned the Coke bottles to the Dasus. I grabbed Jordan's bicycle, and the five of us, mbolo and all, started home.

Saturday nights were usually dull. Often the majority of us would be in Blantyre for the weekend, and Jordan, who had Sunday off, would leave after lunch on Saturday for the village with Ida and the children.

This Saturday was unusual. All of us in both houses were home, and so some of us planned to get together after dinner for pinochle and a little beer drinking and maybe a walk up to Manda's. It was to be a very simple evening, but having spent nearly four weeks alone during the recent teachers' vacation, I was excited about having something to do. To make the day even better, Doug and Mike and John and I, who had all begun to play rugby on a newly formed team in Blantyre and who enjoyed athletics generally, played basketball for several hours on our homemade court. It seemed to be a perfect day in our little community, and I felt at home and comfortable.

At six o'clock, as the sun went down, the lamps were started. The dinner table had been neatly set as it was every night, with a tablecloth and the odds and ends of silverware and plates and cups that we had. It may have seemed strange for young bachelors to eat so formally, but Jordan had established the system, and we had learned to enjoy the routine.

Dan and Mike were seated at the table as I took my seat. Bastone soon joined us. He carried a bowl of soup in one hand and a small plate with a sandwich on it in the other, and so he slid out a chair with his foot and sat down on the end opposite Dan. He steadfastly refused to share in the running of the household and continued to prepare his meals in his room, but he did eat with us, and I enjoyed his company.

Dan reached for a new loaf of Jordan's homemade bread and began to slice off four thick pieces. These were then converted into two peanut-butter sandwiches and quickly eaten. Dan had a huge appetite, and Mike and I often sat in amazement as he ate his appetizers, the size of a meal for most people.

"What's for dinner?" Dan asked to anyone who would answer.

"I don't know," Mike said politely. I simply shrugged my shoulders.

"Jordan," Dan yelled through the kitchen door. "What's for dinner?"

Jordan came running. He leaned through the doorway. "Sir?" He looked to Dan.

"What's for dinner?" Dan repeated.

"It is the pork roast," Jordan answered.

"Good. I'm hungry. Did you get any apples to go with it?"

"No, sir. There are no apples to the market these days," Jordan explained and waited to see if there were more questions.

"Well, what about vegetables?" Dan inquired.

"I am sorry, sir, but there is just the potatoes. And I have managed to buy the green beans. But it is just a little bit."

"How come? This is all we ever have. It's the same everyday," Dan complained.

"Well, I am sorry, but this is all there can be," Jordan answered.

"But why?"

Jordan glanced my way and then answered, "Because the vegetables do not come to this time. And so there can be none."

"But can't you figure out something? There must be some vegetables around, out in the villages someplace. Hell, you have a full-time job. You could scout around, walk out in the villages. Make contacts." Dan hesitated only a moment and went on, "You're just lazy. If it's not in the market, then you're not going to try. You don't care if we get vegetables or not."

"Is this so?" Jordan's tone left no doubt that he did not like Dan's remarks.

"Yeah, this is so," Dan came right back. "And what's for dessert, anyway?"

"I am sorry, sir, but there is no dessert this night." Jordan's voice was soft, but his face was stern, and he glared at Dan.

"See, what did I tell you? You could have made dessert. OK, there's no vegetables, even though I think there are. But a dessert you can make. You can always make some cakes or something and pour some of that treacle molasses over it. Right?" Before Jordan could answer, he continued, "What did you do all afternoon? After lunch, you just went home and sat around. You could have come back and made dessert. You should have done it. Tell me, what did you do all afternoon?"

Jordan was furious, but he held himself in control. Softly he answered, "I have been with Ida and the children. And I can be ironing the clothes."

"Whose clothes? Yours or ours? Yours, right? And whose iron did you use? Ours, right?"

"Knock it off, will you, Dan?" I spoke up. "Who the hell cares if he uses our iron? And he's off every afternoon. God, he starts at five o'clock in the morning. He's got to live too, you know."

"So why didn't he make dessert? It would only take him a half-hour. He could have come back early."

"Forget it, Dan," Mike said. "So there's no dessert. Who cares?"

"I care. He's just being lazy."

"Look, Dan. I was in the market today, and I think Jordan's right. There's really nothing there."

"You always stick up for Jordan. Both of you do. He could have made dessert with what's here. And you know it." As Dan directed himself to us now, Jordan stepped back into the kitchen. He was enraged.

"I know Jordan doesn't like me much, but the feeling's mutual. But he's working for me too. I pay one-third of his salary, and I have a right to say what he does." Dan continued his attack.

"Well, what do you want him to do, asshole? He works all day long. He's a good cook, but he can't make something out of nothing." I was becoming heated now. Some months ago I had beaten Dan in a fistfight, much to the amusement of my roommates, who allowed the fight to linger on and who pulled me away from Dan only when it seemed I might seriously hurt him. I suspected Dan knew he might get the same treatment again if he pushed me too far. "Tell me, don't you think he works enough? God, he's not a machine. So what's the big deal that he didn't make a dessert? Eat some more goddamn peanut butter and bread if you're hungry."

"There you go, automatically sticking up for him." Dan pointed to me as he spoke, and I told him, my voice rising in pitch, that if he pointed at me again, I'd break his finger off.

Mike spoke up to ease the tension, "What's the trouble anyway? It's just that you're a little hungry, right? So you're taking it out on him."

Dan turned to Mike. "I want better food, and he could get it if he wasn't so lazy. Why do we have to eat the same thing every day?"

"Because that's all there is. There is no other food around," Mike explained what seemed obvious. He continued, "Why don't you admit it? You just don't like Jordan for some reason. Right?"

"Right."

"How come, then?" Mike asked.

"I just don't, that's all."

"Come on, you've got to have a reason," Mike pressed him.

Dan hesitated. He searched for the correct words. "Well, he's an arrogant little bastard. He's cheeky." Dan used a British word that was fairly new to our vocabulary. To be cheeky was to have too much cheek, to be mouthy; and it was a highly insulting term in Malawi, where being polite was so important. I knew Jordan was listening from the kitchen and that he would be deeply offended.

"How can you say he's arrogant? Because he likes to look nice? How can you say that?" Mike pushed Dan for a fuller explanation.

"OK, then. He's always trying to be fancy. Heck, he dresses better than we do. What's he trying to prove, anyway? He's just a cook, for God's sake. And he tries to be some big bwana or something."

"Why could you possibly care if he wants to look nice? What harm does it do you?" I was becoming heated again. "Are you telling me you don't dress up sometimes? What are you saying—that poor people have no right to look nice? That they can't spend their money the way they want?"

"Come on. Jordan blows his money on clothes, and he should be saving it. How long is this job going to last? Then what? He could be out of a job for a long time. So he should be saving some money," Dan expanded on his views.

"I can't believe you, you arrogant son of a bitch!" I spoke with growing hostility, and my face, I sensed, was becoming red. "You sit here and pass judgment on this poor bastard who has nothing, not a pot to piss in, nothing, as if you've got all the answers, as if you know what's right. First of all, it's none of your goddamn business how he spends his money. And second, it doesn't make much sense for him to even try to save money. He's got so little in the first place that there's nothing to save. He's just surviving. So don't pass judgment on a guy who takes a little pride in himself."

Dan was not through. "I don't care how much he saves. It's just that he has something. He can live a long time even if he has only a little, and you know it.''

"Dan, the real issue, and *you* know it, is that you don't like him because he's a proud guy. Now admit it. You want him to be stoop-shouldered and to cower to you all the time. You know this. You're the problem, not him." I was regaining my composure, beginning to think things through. My attacking Dan shifted the focus from Jordan and got to the heart of the matter. I continued, "So when all's said and done, you're the asshole, the arrogant bastard, not him. Right, guys?" I looked to Mike and Bastone for support. Mike nodded and Bastone, who had stayed out of our heated discussion, smiled to signal his agreement.

"Bullshit. I'm not trying to be superior to Jordan or anyone else. It's just that he's different. You say it's pride. I say it's arrogance. So that's the difference in how we see it, period. OK?" Dan tried to stop the discussion.

"Isn't it funny you're the only one who sees it this way? Can't you grant the guy a little pleasure? Hell, he's only wearing nice clothes, and besides we gave him most of the stuff anyway." I spoke softly for the first time. I had lots more to say about the matter; but in the interest of keeping peace in our little household, I decided to let it drop. Bastone seemed relieved, and he pulled the bowl of soup closer to himself and began to eat. Mike stood up and went into the kitchen. He made a comment about how good things smelled, and I saw him put his arm around Jordan and hug him. Dan and I simply looked past each other.

It turned out to be a very quiet meal for all of us.

Chapter Eight

A Sense of Place

The trip from Gowa Mission to Jordan's village was now an easy one, since the Peace Corps had purchased a small motorbike for Mike and me. I drove to the dusty crossroads at Mphephozinai, where I made an inquiry of an old man as to the location of Magola village. I had been to Jordan's village once before, but the path was narrow, and it branched several times to neighboring villages and to their gardens. With directions clarified, I drove the remaining distance, less than two miles, making only one error, which I easily corrected. Once in the village, I drove the little motorbike straight to Jordan's hut.

I was immediately surrounded by as many as ten children, and this number quickly tripled as word of my arrival, aided by the sound of the motorbike, spread. Ida was standing in front of the house holding a long, thick wooden pestle. She was pounding maize in the wooden mortar, and two of her older daughters were helping her. The sun was hot, and she was sweating heavily and seemed happy to stop.

The village was similar to dozens I had visited and to hundreds I had passed. The square mud houses, their roofs of grass extending out four feet or so on all sides to form the little khondes where the people could sit or work protected from the sun or the rain, were clustered close together, and the surrounding gardens set the houses off neatly as discrete communities. The houses were placed irregularly, at odd angles to each other, but with sufficient space between each to allow the occupants room to work at their chores, to dry maize kernels on the ground, and to have living space and a modicum of privacy. Some were clustered in grass-walled enclosures where a family, usually sisters and their husbands, had formed a social unit known as a *mbvumba* by taking up a common residence of extended family members. Most houses had no windows. The walls of the huts were of smooth gray clay spread over either sun-dried clay bricks or over loose clay that had been packed between the vertical and cross poles to form the inner structure of the walls. Since the mud would dry and flake off or be washed away by the heavy rains, walls were in constant need of patching.

Between the houses, usually at the back, were the strong woven reed storage bins, or *nkhokwe*, which contained the harvested maize, the fruits of the labor of all these small farmers. These large round containers, some five feet in diameter and eight feet tall, sat a foot or so off the ground on sturdy little platforms of branches to protect the contents from water, rot, and rodents. They were capped with large removable cones of straw that were lifted with care and with considerable effort from the nkhokwe whenever the contents were retrieved.

The enclosed latrines, or chimbudzi, were between the homes and, like the nkhokwe, they were set back and away from the houses. These simple structures, a wall of reeds placed in a rectangle of five or six feet on a side, had no doors, but just a single grass interior wall to block the view from the outside. Unfortunately, these latrines were not deep pits but were simply shallow holes containing large stones on which the users could stand above the excrement. They filled quickly and had to be rebuilt regularly. They were smelly, vile, and nasty to be near and were a source of disease, a blight in the environment that the villagers were forced to endure.

The village was a place alive. Chickens strutted about freely, their heads snapping down and back, their beaks searching almost frantically and at random for anything edible from the bare ground. Goats wandered about, their droppings left underfoot so that you could not forget them. They bleated and arrogantly stared at you, their ears erect, their faces giving no messages, then strolled or sprinted off to find their next mouthful from the stingy environment.

The village was a creation of people, a human community set uncomfortably in nature, the place where their desperate struggle was waged. Simple and basic, primitive in its physical form with grass, mud, dirt, animals, and plants touching and rubbing against each other, it was all manipulated and controlled by the people with great effort and wisdom. People were always in view, sweeping the ground with crude straw brooms to keep things tidy, pounding maize, washing clothes in metal buckets or hanging clothes to dry on little bushes or on lines strung between the huts, hauling water on their heads in giant clay pots, cooking nsima, and washing dishes. Women sat on the ground before their homes with neighbors and their babies and prepared vegetables or sewed clothes or just chatted. Men and women and teenagers, tired and hot from their hard labors, returned from the fields to wash and clean themselves. Children played tag and hide-and-seek or busied themselves with little homemade toys. They would organize little soccer games with tightly tied balls of grass or, if lucky, with an old tennis ball. Old women slept on the khondes, boys wrestled, teens flirted, people visited and laughed with one another and sometimes argued too. It was a complete world, a little tenuous perhaps, but full of vitality, as all basic human activities were found here. Life was in the open, social, and easily observable for the most part, although politics and private affairs were submerged and hidden from the short-term visitor. One could comprehend the community working and imagine it as enjoyable and fulfilling, the basis of the psychological well-being of its inhabitants.

I dismounted from the motorbike and leaned it against a pole that supported the khonde's roof. Ida stepped forward smiling, and I greeted her and her two girls. Then I shook hands with all the kids, even the babies who were being held by their big sisters. Jordan came running. He was nicely dressed, with shoes shined and trousers pressed and his long-sleeved white shirt and striped tie. His clothes, when compared with the drab and faded clothes of the kids, seemed to sparkle. He actually looked opulent, for only a rich man could have such clothes without holes and so neatly cleaned and pressed. I wondered what the villagers thought of a cook, a man with a steady income, a man who could dress so well, a man who spent most of his time away from the village.

"Hello, boss. I am sorry to be late," Jordan said, his breath a little short. "I have been inspecting the garden to the other side. When I heard the motorbike, I came as soon as possible."

"No problem, achimwene. I'm all done at Gowa, so there's no rush. If you're not ready to leave yet, I can just hang around. So don't hurry."

Jordan thought for a moment. "Well, perhaps you can like to inspect my house. I can make so many improvements to this time. Just a little bit."

"Sure. Whatever you'd like to do. And I wouldn't mind seeing your gardens if you'd like to show them to me," I said.

"Oh, that can be jolly nice. We can walk to the gardens now if that is the wish of my boss." Jordan seemed pleased. He spoke quickly to Ida, who listened to him carefully. I guessed he was explaining our upcoming tour and was giving her some other instructions about the remainder of my visit. The children began to run in the direction from which Jordan had just come. Like kids everywhere, they were excited to have a visitor in their midst and they wanted to lead the tour and show me that they knew the way.

Jordan and I and perhaps fifteen of the smaller children set off, passing nine or ten houses, and I greeted every adult as I moved along with the entourage. We moved through a large stand of plantains and past a small patch of cassava plants and then walked through a little woods of some type of deciduous tree that likely served as an important source of firewood for the people in the area. The ground here was picked clean of branches and twigs, and the little forest gave the appearance of being neat and tidy. The people knew the value of these trees, and no one would cut them down without a great deal of criticism. Finally, we came to an opening where one rolling field joined another for a quarter of a mile in all directions.

Jordan took the lead, and we walked along a series of footpaths between the maize, now about waist high, until we came upon a boy of perhaps fourteen. The boy stood at attention when he heard the commotion of our excited band of inspectors. He held a traditional short-handled hoe, or *khasu*, used by farmers throughout the central and southern regions of Malawi. It was a homemade affair. The handle was cut from the branch of a tree where it intersected the tree trunk, and a flat steel blade, purchased at an Indian shop, was inserted like an adze at ninety degrees to the line of the handle. The boy had been weeding, and the sweat around his ankles and hands was mixed with dirt.

Jordan stopped suddenly before reaching him, and the children gathered around us. He began to tell me about the garden, how far it reached, when he began planting, how he was nervous that the rains would not continue after they had begun. He walked across a few rows of the maize and inspected the leaves and the little tassels that were beginning to form. He explained how he had mixed some beans in with the maize so that the maize itself could be used as a support for this climbing plant. His good garden, he explained, was due to his ability to utilize fertilizer, and his job as a cook was the key to purchasing it. He pointed to some neighboring fields where fertilizer had not been used, and I could easily see how these gardens were inferior to his.

He was obviously enjoying himself, and like most farmers he could have talked at great length about his little plot of ground. He appeared happy. He stood and looked, then walked a little, and looked some more. This little garden constituted the basis of his survival, and his keen interest in it was understandable. For the moment it commanded all his attention.

"So your garden's a good one. It's doing well, then?" I spoke up and broke his concentration.

"It is a little like that, boss."

"So you're happy, then. It seems to be coming along OK? I can't tell, but it looks pretty good."

"Yes, it is OK, but the rains are not so fine." Things were never perfect for a farmer—too much rain, not enough rain, too hot, too cold, too many insects, too many monkeys—but it appeared overall that it would be a good crop and that he was pleased.

"Who's this boy working here?" I asked.

"Oh, he is just a village boy," Jordan answered.

"Is he working for you?"

"Yes, boss. I hired him to cultivate. He can be helping my Ida because I am to the job with my bosses."

"So you're the big bwana with an employee. Pretty fancy."

"No, boss. He is just a young chap. He can receive just these few pennies. These young boys they do this. As you know, my boss, many of the big men are to South Africa to the mines. And so these boys do the cultivating."

"Pretty good system, then."

"Well, it is what we must do." Jordan took a last look at his garden. "So, we can be going because we have too many miles to the boma." Jordan never introduced me to the young man.

I followed Jordan and the children back to the village, and Jordan glanced back at the garden several times as we walked. Ida, three other women, and a man about fifty years old were standing before Jordan's house when we arrived. Jordan introduced the man first. He was the village headman, and it was his job to keep track of all events in the community. He spoke no English, so I did what I could at making small talk. Having worked in many villages, I no longer felt awkward with these conversations, but my Chichewa was still so elementary that we simply talked about the weather and the state of the gardens. I probably appeared simple-minded, but village people were so polite that they would never show disrespect.

The women were introduced next. Two were neighbors, and one was Ida's sister, holding a baby on her hip.

"Would you like to come into the house, boss?" Jordan asked after our greetings. "I should like you to see my house again."

The tour of the little two-room home began. Jordan pushed the wooden door open, and I stepped forward, ducking my head as I passed through the doorway until I stood in the larger of the two rooms, which contained a table, two chairs, and three clay pots, which rested on the dirt floor. There was a green cardboard suitcase lying on its side, and three metal cups, knives, forks, and spoons, and a can opener were resting on it. Twine had been placed across the far corner of the room, and several of Ida's dresses and a few of Jordan's pants and shirts, all on hangers, were hung from the makeshift clothesline. On the floor along one wall were a small box of Surf soap powder, several small batteries that seemed to have no purpose, a burlap bag of maize kernels, and a small iron, the type that is heated from fire coals. For a man as neat and clean as Jordan, I knew this was an important household item.

The other room, Jordan explained, was where the children slept, and it was practically empty too. Grass sleeping mats had been rolled up and stood along the back wall of the house. Several blankets and a small pile of children's clothes, all folded neatly, had been placed on a mat in the corner, but this was all. It seemed to me that Jordan's and Ida's possessions were almost nonexistent, and yet I knew most other villagers possessed even less. Jordan had additional clothing and blankets and a radio in his room at our house, and more importantly he did have food, even at this time of the year before the new crops were harvested. We in the West possessed far more than we reasonably needed. But I did not wish to have less than I had, and Jordan, who worked so hard to provide for his family, could never be convinced that there was any merit in living so simply.

"Come, boss, to the outside. I will show you the new articles." Jordan bid me to step out on the khonde. "Do you see, boss?" Jordan asked.

"What, Jordan? What am I looking at?"

"The windows. These are the new windows that the carpenter has made. They have glass and the new wooden frames of which I have spoken to you. So now there is the window to each room. It is too lovely for the house."

"Oh, of course. I forgot all about the new windows. I'm sorry. And that's why the rooms were so bright and nice when we were inside. When did you get them?"

Jordan touched the windows and ran his fingers over the new frames. There were six panes in two rows of three, and the unpainted wood was obviously new. "The carpenter has just completed this one. And look, boss, the windows open to get the good air in the house." He moved the window, which hinged on the side, for me to see.

"They're really nice. You must be happy with them. I can see what an improvement they are." I swung the window in and out a few times and smiled to show my approval, to share in his enthusiasm. "So what other home improvements do you plan, Jordan?"

"Well, I am liking the iron sheets to the roof but to this time they are very dear. I just cannot afford. And so I must just use the grass as you can see."

The tour was over, and Jordan ordered Ida to get his things together. Ida in turn spoke to her oldest daughter, who ran inside the house. She soon returned with a small basket containing a plastic bag full of maize flour. This would keep Jordan supplied until Ida joined him later in the week. Jordan's little son, Flanki, whom I often played with at our house, stepped forward from the crowd and presented me with a live chicken. Flanki was small and the chicken was large in comparison, and the many onlookers smiled as they saw little Flanki, following his parents' orders, make the presentation.

Several times I had received gifts like chickens or vegetables when I visited villages. It was difficult for me to accept presents because their economic value meant so little to me and presumably so much to the givers. The need to give, to express oneself through giving, seemed obvious, however, and so I always met my obligation and accepted the gifts. Yet never did I feel comfortable doing so. I took the chicken from Flanki and, holding it in one hand against my chest, I reached down and shook his hand and thanked him. Embarrassed, he looked to Ida for help as the women in the group smiled in sympathy. I reached down and touched his head and ran my fingers through his hair, and then I passed the chicken over to Jordan. I reached in the pocket of my shorts and took out all the money I had, about fourteen shillings, and handed it to Flanki. I told him to buy all the children a Coke from the shop, which I knew must exist somewhere nearby. He was confused but held the money tightly and looked to his father for help. Jordan translated my instructions slowly to him, but he looked to the older children, who would surely be managing the money as soon as the adults were no longer present. The glances and smiles of the children in the crowd told me they were excited, but they were too polite to run off to the store before I departed.

I knew the money I had given little Flanki would cause some problems. It was not enough for everyone to get a drink, so there would need to be some sharing that might lead to arguments and a few tears, especially on the part of the little ones, but I thought the risk was worth it. These kids deserved a little treat, some fun and excitement, and I hoped I did not appear arrogant or patronizing with the way I so easily passed over the money. A man in this village would work for more than a week to earn as much and to spend it on Cokes, something frivolous when so much else was needed, could appear wasteful. The joy in the kids' faces made it clear that they were not about to analyze the situation, and the expressions of the mothers were approving as best I could tell. Their children had the right to a little enjoyment, and they seemed to take pleasure in knowing the children were happy and excited. Perhaps I was being too sensitive. It was a simple gesture, after all. If there was any arrogance, perhaps it was in my thinking that the people might regard me as generous in the first place.

"Say, Jordan," I spoke softly as I climbed on the motorbike. "I don't think I should take this chicken. I don't want to be rude because it's very nice of you and Ida to give it to me. But we can buy lots of chickens when we get home. Why don't you just keep it? It would be better that way. What do you think?" I was taking a risk, but I guessed that Jordan would understand that I was not refusing his gift as much as thinking of his family, who could use the food.

He looked at me for a moment, and I was afraid I had gravely insulted him and his family. He looked quickly to Ida, who had not understood me, and then accepted my suggestion. Jordan spoke to Ida and passed the chicken over to her. He then spoke to his daughter, who ran off to return a minute later with two small eggs. Then he explained as best I could tell to the women why the chicken was being exchanged for the eggs. He seemed to say the chicken would be too difficult to transport, while the eggs we could carry easily. It was a good story and benefited us all.

Jordan climbed on the back of the motorbike, and the basket was handed to him. The two eggs were put in with the flour, and the plastic bag was knotted and closed again. Jordan said a few words to everyone and then gave Ida a few last instructions. I waved to the kids, and we started down the path to Mphephozinai and to the dirt road home. The children ran before us until they tired of the game.

The small motorbike strained with the additional weight, and I was forced to drive slowly. The dirt road was rough, rocky, and pot-holed; even a lorry would have had a difficult time. I simply followed the bicycle path, which meandered independently of the road, and this greatly smoothed out the ride.

We passed two more villages, and Jordan waved to a number of people, who waved in return. We then crossed a large open field of short grass that stretched a half a mile in each direction. The field contained no gardens. It was an area for grazing the Ngoni's cattle, and as we crossed I caught sight of one small herd of eight or nine cattle and three little shepherd boys of about ten years of age. The three of them turned and stared as we passed through their field. I gave them a quick wave, and their hands immediately shot up in reply. I wondered how the lives of these boys and their families differed from those of the other villagers. Were they better off? Did cattle still give one status and prestige as they once had? Could you also have gardens if you had cattle? Was shepherding as difficult as it seemed in this area without fences and with so many cultivated fields? Oddly, I knew no cattle owners and guessed that there probably were not many left. The area was heavily populated, and the demands on the land were obvious, as even steep hillsides were planted, and maize often grew within a few feet of people's homes. The cattle must occupy a narrow niche in this delicate system, their numbers kept in check, their location controlled carefully by the boys.

Through the field, we began the long climb to the main road, which would take us to Mphate and then home. The Ntcheu district sloped, like most of Malawi, from the west to Lake Malawi in the east. Our home was to the west of Jordan's village, so the ride was a strenuous uphill climb, and the motorbike was not up to the task. We came without any warning, without a sputter or a backfire, to a quiet and complete stop. Our efforts to start the bike failed repeatedly, and with no other options we began to take turns pushing the bike and carrying Jordan's basket. Because the path was steep and the sun very hot, the bike seemed to get heavier and heavier. In a quarter of a mile we were sweating; at one mile we were panting and lathered in sweat; and by three miles we were completely spent. We had nothing left, and yet we trudged on. I lost confidence that the two of us were capable of completing the trip.

Mercifully, a large mango tree, its green leaves leathery and dense, stood by the side of the road. Its offer of shade was overwhelming and Jordan, who was now pushing, wheeled the bike without discussion under the low branches and set it upright. The two of us flopped down, exhausted. We leaned against the tree trunk and said nothing for a long time, fifteen minutes or more. I did regain my breath but could not seem to cool down, and the perspiration continued to pour from my forearms and legs. Jordan seemed to be doing no better, and he just stared along the road and over the long slope we had just climbed to the field with the shepherd boys in the distance and to his village beyond that.

"Jordan, how are you doing?" I spoke to break our long silence.

"Oh, boss, I am too tired and very much sweating. Ah, it is too hot. And this motorbike is very heavy to push."

"You're right about being hot and about the bike too." I took a few more breaths and turned to him. "Look, I've got an idea. I don't think we're ever going to get the stupid bike home, unless we kill ourselves. So what we can do is hire someone to push it home. What do you think about that? Maybe two young guys, and they could take their time. Do it in the evening when it's cool or take two days even. Good idea?"

"This can be, boss. There are so many people who pass to this road. I am sure they can do this job. Yes, it can be possible." Jordan was delighted with the plan.

"Then all we have to do is sit here until someone comes by, in either direction, and ask him. Somebody will do it," I said. "How much do you think it's worth? Ten shillings?"

"Oh no. I should say two shillings, or one and six, but not ten, my boss. No, this can be too much," Jordan protested. Men in this area generally received two and six for a whole day's work, so Jordan's pricing was based on this rate and his assumption that the trip would take less than a day.

"But there's maybe eight or ten miles to go, and it's all uphill. It's a tough job. We both know that. Look, when someone comes along, just offer him ten shillings. There will be no hassles that way. The hell with the money. OK?"

Jordan agreed reluctantly, and I knew he thought I was wasting my money. He always protected me and bargained hard on my behalf and would want to strike a fair deal now. There was nothing to do but to wait, so I leaned back and closed my eyes.

"Boss?"

"What, Jordan?"

"Did you like the visit to the village?"

"Of course. It's a nice place. Real nice. And the people are friendly too."

"Is it, boss? The people are friendly?"

"Sure. Don't you like the village?" I began to take an interest in our conversation and sat up straight, my eyes open.

"Well, yes, boss. It is my home, my place, you know this. I like the Magola village. It is where my children are growing and where my gardens are located. It is the place for your Jordan and my Ida."

"Well, what's best, the village or the boma or Blantyre? Where would you like to live if you could choose, the village or in town?"

"The village, boss. I am just the farmer, a peasant, and this is the place to this earth for me. It is where the people are and the land for the maize."

"Wait a minute, Jordan. Let's say you had lots of money. You were a big bwana with a fancy car and could buy a big house in Blantyre and have lots of servants. Understand? Where would you like to live then?"

"But I cannot be having the money," Jordan protested.

"I know. But *if* you had lots of money. If you did. Then what? Would you live in town or here?"

"I cannot imagine, my boss. This cannot be."

"I'm just asking you to imagine, to pretend you had lots of money. I know you're not going to get it, but it's like a game. If you were rich, where would you live?"

"But I cannot have the money. It is not for small people such as we village people. So I cannot just say, boss."

I tried a new tactic. "OK. Let's just say then that you were a boy at a shop. Or maybe you worked for the government as a postal clerk, or maybe you were a lorry driver. Then where would you live?"

Jordan looked at me. His face lit up. "I could be a lorry driver, boss, this I know. I am clever to the machines, yes, true. Can you help me to get a license for being a lorry driver?"

"Jordan, I don't even have a car, so how can I get you a license? I'd do it but I can't. You know that." I hoped I was not being rude, but Jordan understood me well enough now to know I would help in any way I could. I returned to the quiz. "Pretend you had a good job in town, any job, it doesn't matter. Would you rather do that or be here in the village?"

Jordan thought, and I watched him closely as he pondered the question. "I can live to the village. I should like to have a very big garden such as these big farmers with so many crops. This and that, what, what. This can be too wonderful. The crops for the food and for a little selling for the money. I can have the money for the school fees and for the nice clothing for the children and Ida. I can have a little pocket money and a very powerful radio, the kind that you cannot buy here to Ntcheu, but only to Blantyre. This is what I should like." He turned to me as he finished.

"Why?" I inquired further, perhaps unfairly. Jordan simply looked at me, the wrinkles in his forehead and the squint around his eyes indicating either his confusion or his feeling that this was a ridiculous question, his dreams having been sufficiently explained.

"Why, boss?" He thought for a long while and appeared a little embarrassed that he had no quick answer. "Because it is the village. It is the place of the people. The gardens for our food are here and this is how we can live. The village can be the place for our living."

"I understand, Jordan. I'm just curious. I know it's a tough question." I tried to soften the discussion and to remove him from my little spotlight. "What I am really asking is what makes you happy, but maybe you've already answered that."

"Happy. To be happy, boss, is this what you are wishing to know?"

"That's it. Like you said, it's a big garden and lots of food and some money and things for the kids. And you'd like to live in the village too. That's it, right?"

Jordan looked straight at me. It was a curious look, again with a little embarrassment, but this time it was mixed with a little wonder, a little confusion. He turned at last and looked out over the plain below us. His face was strangely blank and without emotion, but his nostrils flared ever so slightly; and his mind seemed to race in an attempt to sort out the question, to grasp its meaning, its magnitude. I began to feel uneasy. He had no obligation to tell me his dreams, and perhaps I should end our discussion. And it was a difficult question. Most people would have great trouble even beginning to answer it, but my curiosity was piqued—what was the scope of his dreams for himself? Did he even have any?—and so I waited for his reply.

"Well, boss, I do not know what to say," he began quietly. "These things I have told you, as I have said, are the things for a man such as me. It is the food for the family which we must have. This is the basic thing. Then there can be the house and the clothes. These are the things we are just needing." He paused a moment but went on. "If we have a little bit of money this is good, for the school fees and better clothing and for some goods to make the life better. I am just a simple chap, and these can be the things for me."

"But you like to wear nice clothes, and you want to put iron sheets on your roof, and you'd like to own a bicycle, right? So you do want more things, which is fair." I spoke softly and, I hoped, in a way which indicated my understanding. "I suppose what I am asking is why you don't want bigger things. You know, like a big house even if it is here in the village, or a big job where you can make thousands of pounds a year. Things like that."

"This can be too good, boss. This is true. But these things they are not for me. They cannot be." He spoke matter-of-factly, simply stating what he knew to be true about his life. There seemed to be no bitterness or regret in his voice. He had come to a realistic assessment of his state in life and seemed to have accepted it. We both sat quietly for several minutes and said nothing.

I spoke again, "What about the kids? What do you see for them?"

Jordan looked over at me. "This is difficult. The school fees are the most big problem for me to pay. The oldest daughter, the one we have just visited, she missed this year to school because there is no money. And the sons to my previous marriage, they went to Standard Three only and they are just staying with their mother, the previous wife as I have said, to the village. So this can be the problem." He thought some more. "My children can just stay to the village. Well, they must do the best that they can do. It is too difficult these days. I know the schooling is important, but what can I do?"

I was saddened by what I heard. I had assumed Jordan was better off than most villagers and that somehow all his children were in school, but I had been insensitive in not finding out sooner. The schools, particularly the rural schools, were staffed almost exclusively by unqualified teachers who had not gone much beyond the fifth or sixth standard themselves. The education surely was poor, but for the brightest or most motivated it did offer a chance. "It's not very fair is it, Jordan?" I asked.

"What do you mean fair, my boss?"

"Fair. You know. Some people have so much, and others have so little. Some can't send their kids to school, and others can, easily. You know what I mean?"

"Well, it can be not fair to us but I am understanding what you mean. This world it seems to be a difficult place, this I know. The people are just these little farmers and that is the way it is. The way the God has made the world."

"You think God made the world to have lots of poor people and a few rich ones?"

"Well, it seems to be the way. This I know."

"So then God isn't fair. I mean if He can't even give people enough money to send their kids to school. Is that what they teach over at Gowa Mission?" The conversation shifted away from the notion of fairness.

"Ah, I do not know about these mission people, boss. I do not go there as I told you long ago. It is a no good place for they are always telling the people what to do and to behave this way and that. And they are taking the people's money for this and that." I had observed that Jordan seemed to have little interest in organized religion, or at least in formal Western Christian churches, which were quite common in Malawi. His worldview, which he attributed at least in part to God, seemed to be just a casual expression that rationalized the inequalities that he knew existed and with which he seemed resigned.

"Say, Jordan, let me tell you a funny story. Well, actually it's sad, I guess." Jordan looked at me intently. "Today I went to Gowa before I came to get you. I went to see the Sister there who runs the little clinic, where I see the TB patients."

"Yes, boss, I know this place."

"You know what they did? They sacked the lab assistant. This man had been going to the mission for many years. In fact, he went to school there as a boy. Over the past two years they trained him to work in the clinic, and he seemed to be pretty good to me. Anyway, they sacked him last Friday."

"Oh no, boss," Jordan's voice showed real concern. Jobs were scarce, and he naturally sympathized with anyone who lost one. "Why is this?"

"She said, and this is the sad part, because he was drinking in the villages. They trained him for two years and fired him because he was drinking."

"This can be too stupid, boss. But these people are such as this.

I know. For drinking, oh, it is too crazy." He shook his head.

"I agree, especially since beer drinking is a part of village life." I continued, "But the stupid part is that I have a little hangover right now. We were all drinking last night, and I am still full of beer. So if she knew this, she would probably sack me from coming to the mission too. Funny business, huh?"

Jordan did not laugh. The bit of humor I saw in the situation either missed him or seemed insignificant when compared to the man's misfortune, and so he said nothing.

Five minutes passed. Jordan finally spoke up, "Say, boss. What is it that makes you happy?"

I turned to him, "Hell, I don't know. That's too hard a question. I guess it's girlfriends. Lots of girlfriends make me happy."

"Girlfriends?"

"Yeah, girlfriends. Women. Lots of beautiful women, that's what we need. And some beer, too. That's happiness. Right?"

Jordan looked at me very intently. "The women are the happiness? I do not think, boss. Is this true?"

"God, Jordan. You know I'm kidding you by now. I don't know what happiness is. You've probably got it right. At the moment I'd settle for a couple of sons of bitches to come along and push this goddamn motorbike." Jordan laughed. Our wonderful conversation seemed to be ending in silliness, as they often did. I hoped he was not angered because I took his inquiries less seriously than he had taken mine, but in my young view there would always be more time for conversations.

Good fortune arrived soon. Jordan spotted two well-built teenage boys, one of whom he knew, and he hired them for the task. They seemed delighted with the arrangement and were big enough for the job.

The four of us started off together, Jordan carrying our basket for the first stretch. The boys soon fell behind, and Jordan and I walked alone.

"Jordan, I forgot to ask you. Are you happy now?"

"Oh yes, my boss. The things are too wonderful these days. Too wonderful."

The long walk turned out to be a pleasant one.

Chapter Nine

Growing Watermelons

"You look horrible, Jordan. I can't believe your eyes. They look like road maps." John winked and slowly shook his head side to side as he spoke, and Mike and I forced a laugh that contained a little sympathy. Lester and Robert just looked at poor Jordan, but they seemed to understand John's comment as a good-natured one.

"Hell, the son of a bitch just got up and it's almost ten o'clock. He was completely snookered last night, drank the bar dry, drank everything in Ntcheu. They'll have to send a lorry to Blantyre today to get some more beer," Mike continued the razz, and now Lester and Robert joined us in the laugh.

Jordan looked sheepishly at the five of us seated around the dining room table. "Is this so? No, it is not. I am fine. I am just a bit tired from my duties," he spoke but fooled no one.

"Come on, Jordan, why don't you admit it? You're not tired. You're just hung over from too much partying. Isn't he hung over, Robert?" I tapped Robert on the arm and pointed to Jordan.

"Too much. This one drink too many beers to the whole night. He is a too bloody drunk one. Ah, no." Robert was loving this friendly put-down and was glad to support us. He switched to Chichewa, and his voice rose, and he started to speak very rapidly. Lester burst into laughter at whatever was said, and the three of us joined in because it seemed appropriate. Suddenly Robert stood up and began staggering around the room pretending he was drunk. Then he stopped and pointed at Jordan, and he and Lester laughed even harder. I stood up and joined him, and soon John and Mike joined us. Round and round we staggered. We bumped into the table and each other and pretended to run into the walls. We laughed,

101

pointed at Jordan, and observed Lester, who was convulsed in laughter. It was a silly scene and Jordan, who had tried to be above it, to maintain his innocence, finally broke down and joined with us.

When things settled down, I went to the kitchen to get Jordan a cup of coffee. He was seated with the others when I returned, and, like theirs, his face still showed the effects of the hearty laughter. I placed the cup before him and returned to my seat. "So, achimwene, that was some party we had last night, wasn't it?"

"Oh, yes, it was a too good time. The beer we are having was too much. It can be all gone now, this I know," Jordan answered.

"Well, if you hadn't passed out on us, you could have walked up to Mphate with us, and we could have had some more," Mike said.

Jordan looked surprised. "You went to Mphate, my bosses. Is this true?" Jordan looked to Lester for confirmation. Lester nodded and smiled.

"Yep, we all went. Robert and Lester. All of us. And we had a good time. Of course, I guess you had to get your beauty rest," John said playfully. "I thought you could handle a big celebration, but I guess not."

"We thought you would dance all night with us. It isn't everyday a pain in the ass like Dan leaves, but I guess you weren't as happy as we were," I added.

"No, boss. It is a too good celebration, this I know. But, boss, we have been drinking the beer since that Dan has departed, for the whole afternoon and for the night. I just cannot manage."

"Oh, forget it, Jordan. As long as you had fun, that's all that matters. We could see that you were not long for this world. Hell, by eight o'clock you looked finished," I said.

The conversation among the six of us continued along similar lines. The day before, Dan had departed for the United States, and we were all extremely pleased. He had done a creditable job under difficult conditions as an English teacher at the secondary school, but his relationship with us had been miserable. Our little community was close, and we interacted constantly. Our relationships with one another demanded flexibility and tolerance to make our frequent social intercourse flow easily. Mike and I got out into the community a good deal because our work took us into the villages, but the teachers moved almost exclusively between the school and our two houses; therefore, getting along required sensitivity to others' needs and the willingness to work at being considerate of others. Unfortunately, Dan was incapable of living in such close proximity to other people, especially over long periods of time. He was, by his own admission, selfish and inconsiderate, and our lives suffered accordingly. One major source of annoyance involved his playing a piano that he had found someplace and had shipped to our home. After working on it for months to restore it to some barely playable condition, he began what seemed like an endless elementary practice session. Loud and heavy-handed, he pounded out scales; up and down he would go, over and over, faster and faster. This repetitive noise was interrupted only when he occasionally struggled to play a tune from one of the few pieces of sheet music available to him. To make matters worse, he frequently chose to play late at night because he claimed he could not sleep. He usually ignored our protests that the timing of his recitals was unacceptable and that none of *us* could sleep; we were faced with putting up with him, in the interest of harmony, or, at our wits' end, threatening him with bodily injury. For Jordan and the other Malawians, things were even more difficult. Dan had little understanding of their needs as employees within the job or as men with family obligations outside the job. He distrusted them and was incapable of seeing the complexities of their work or the priorities, planning, and thought that went into it. We were all pleased that he was gone and Jordan, who had celebrated so much the night before, and who had been singularly subjected to Dan's most inconsiderate ways, was the happiest of all.

"So, Jordan, it'll only be another week or two before crazy Bastone leaves with the three kids. Then we'll be getting some new guys to replace them. It'll be nice to have some new faces around here," I said.

"What do you mean the three kids? I do not understand," Jordan asked.

"Didn't you know he was taking three boys with him to the United States when he leaves? You know, the three boys who come over here afternoons after school, Nelson and Lester and Rodney. He's taking them home with him when he leaves."

Jordan looked surprised. "These small boys can go to the United States? They are very lucky indeed, boss." Jordan paused and looked at Robert and Lester as if seeking confirmation. "Who are these boys? They are just these small lads."

John spoke up, "They're three kids in his Form I Mathematics class. He thinks they're smart, and he likes them. He asked them if they wanted to go and then went out to the village where they live and asked their parents. They said OK, so he made all the arrangements. He got them passports and visas and so on. In a couple of weeks they're off."

"These small boys can go to the United States, boss? They are too lucky, isn't this? This is too wonderful." Jordan translated for Robert and Lester, who nodded in agreement.

"And how will they go?" Jordan asked.

"By plane. They'll just fly to London and then to New York. It's easy," Mike explained.

"What about the bus? Is this too far this New York place?"

Mike smiled. "Sure it is. It would take a year to get there by bus. Actually, you can't get there that way. And you'd have to cross over the ocean, so you'd have to fly anyway."

"How far is this place?"

"About nine or ten thousand miles."

"Is this a long way? I should say it is beyond Lilongwe and even Karonga to the north, is this so?"

The three of us smiled, and our Malawian friends stared intently at Mike for his reply.

"It sure is. Lilongwe's about a hundred miles north, and so New York's a hundred times as far. You must travel to Lilongwe from here one hundred times. Let's say one day you take the bus to Lilongwe, and the next day you come back here. Then you do this for fifty days, or about two months. That is how far they must travel."

It was a good explanation. Jordan shook his head and spoke to Robert and Lester, who appeared fascinated with Jordan's own elaborate explanation. Lessons on geography and distance were generally amusing, since most people here spent their entire lives close to their homes. Long trips on foot were difficult, and there was little purpose to travel in the first place. Robert had worked in the mines in South Africa, and Jordan and Lester had worked in Rhodesia, so the explanation was at least partially comprehensible to them.

"Robert wishes to know about London. Where is this? We know so much about this place because of these English people who are coming from there," Jordan asked.

"Where's London? It's about six thousand miles north of here. Just go to Lilongwe and take a slight left, and you'll bump right into it." John answered, and I chuckled.

"So it is very far beyond Malawi then, this I can see." Jordan translated this observation to his compatriots. "It is to the other side of Nairobi then, is this so?"

"Oh, Kenya's close to Malawi, really. It's just two countries north. London's maybe five times as far," Mike continued.

"So this Kenya's close by. I did not know this. Well, I knew it was to Africa. But I do not know where this place is."

"The next country north is Tanzania, then comes Kenya. Actually, it is far away. It's just not very far when you compare it to London or New York. See what I mean?" I said.

"Yes, I think I am seeing this. Kenya is too far, if by footing it is too far. But this London it is to the other side of Kenya and is much distance. As for New York, I cannot imagine." Jordan then went into a long explanation for Robert and Lester, who were polite enough to make a few expressions to indicate some interest. "My Lester here wishes to know about the village of Bastone and if he is having a big garden to this place New York? And what are the crops that these people are growing there?"

"Bastone grows watermelons. He comes from a long line of watermelon growers. In fact, in Italian Bastone means watermelon. That's how he got his name. Didn't you know that?" I continued.

"True, boss. He is growing watermelons?" Jordan looked at me with considerable interest.

"Yep, everyday he gets in his car and drives out to his garden to work on the watermelons. All the Bastones do this together. But they all take their own cars, because in New York everyone has a car, and they like to drive alone."

"This is very interesting. These people can be very fortunate to drive the car to the gardens. They are very rich, I can see this."

"That's nothing. When it rains, they take a subway, which is a train that moves underground, out to their gardens. That way the cars don't get wet. You see, in New York a lot of cars shrink, and so they keep them inside their houses during the rainy season. So that's the way they do it."

Jordan's face broke into a smile. "Oh, my boss is teasing me again. The cars cannot shrink, and this train underground and putting the cars into the houses, this is too funny, boss." Jordan explained my tale to Robert and Lester, and they laughed.

"OK, Jordan, so you're right. I am just kidding. But I'll tell you one thing, and you can ask John and Mike. In New York they don't even have gardens. The whole place is concrete, and some of the buildings are a thousand feet high. Nothing grows there. It's only concrete with people walking around on top of it. It's like a tarmac road and big buildings and maybe a half a dozen trees and that's all. Except the Bastone family grows a few watermelons in a flower pot on the fiftieth floor of their apartment building. Really."

Jordan burst into laughter. "No gardens," he roared, "No gardens. This cannot be. How can the people eat without gardens? So now I know you can be teasing me." Jordan explained to Robert and Lester how he had caught me in a lie, and they howled in laughter at my wild claims.

"OK, so you don't believe me. Well, I'll tell you how they do it. Now what does Bastone eat all the time? He eats sandwiches, right?" I stopped to let them think this over. "In New York, they have these little restaurants all over the place called delicatessens. That's where the people get all their food. They just go in there and eat sandwiches all day long. This is true."

"But, boss, where does the food for these restaurants come from? It can come from the gardens. This I know."

"Not in New York. The government just gives the food to restaurants, and they sell it to the people. Don't ask me where the government gets it. I think they have a few big farms someplace, or maybe they steal it. All I know is that the people just eat sandwiches, and sometimes some of the lucky ones have some watermelon too. At least the ones who know the Bastones get watermelon." I had gone too far. The story was now so absurd that they would believe nothing I said. I gave it one last try nevertheless. "OK, I made it all up except for one thing. The people in New York do drive their own cars out to their garden every morning when they go do their cultivating. This is the only true thing I've told you. Ask John. He lives near New York."

"This is a thing which is too wonderful, this I know. This New York has so many rich people and they can be so happy to be driving to their gardens." Jordan and Robert and Lester started a quiet conversation among themselves to consider the good fortune of the New Yorkers.

"Say, Jordan, do you know where Bastone is now?" Mike asked.

"No. Where is he? I have seen the desks can be missing to his room. So he has taken them. But where?" Jordan had no answer.

"Who knows? He just took all forty of them yesterday and left. Your guess is as good as mine where he went," I said.

"But how is this, boss? These desks are too big and they have the seat to them as well. How can he move them?" Jordan now asked.

"Ask Robert. He saw him doing it." I turned to Robert, "Go on, Robert; tell him what Bastone did," I continued.

"He taked desks to Matope Road just there." Robert turned and pointed to the main road that ran around the outside of the boma area about a quarter-mile from our house. "He and boy from school move desks."

"You mean they took twenty trips each up to the road. That's incredible," Mike said. "Then what did they do?"

"He take bus. Lilongwe bus. I see him," Robert answered.

"You mean he stopped the bus and put forty desks on it? How could he do that?" Mike was astounded.

"To top and some to bus. Too much," Robert continued.

"He put the desks on the roof and then put some in the bus itself. I can't believe this. He's crazier than I thought." Mike's face was a mixture of a frown and a smile. "Where's he taking the stupid things? Is he going to sell them?"

Mike looked at us for an answer, but none of us spoke. Bastone surely had something in mind, but he was an extremely private person and shared little about his life with any of us, even going to the extreme of not asking for help in moving the desks.

Finally Jordan spoke up. "It can be Mtendere Mission above Dedza. He has spoken sometime that he will go to this place."

"Mtendere. Hell, that's ten miles off the main road. How's he going to get them into the mission from the road? If he's done that, he's gone completely crazy. Unbelievable," I commented.

"Well, this is what he has spoken. So I do not know," Jordan shook his head slowly, and we sat for a moment to consider the matter.

Finally, Lester spoke softly to Jordan in Chichewa. He asked for a more complete explanation. Living in the other house, he sometimes missed out on Bastone stories; and because there was a constant flow of them, he found it difficult to follow all of them.

Jordan began to answer, but he turned to me and asked if I could explain it.

"Well, Lester, it seems crazy Bastone somehow got the idea that it would be nice if the classroom he uses at the secondary school has these fancy new desks. For some reason he didn't like the long desks, the ones like tables, which the students used now. He got a book from a company in Rhodesia that sells these things. Then he sent them a check, and some months later they sent the desks. Actually, they came before you started to work here." Lester was paying close attention, and I was enjoying the chance to retell the whole story. "Now what happened is that the desks were left out on the side of the main road, maybe near where he got on the bus yesterday. Anyway, he spent a whole day putting the desks on that little wheelbarrow he has and taking them down to the school. Back and forth, about forty round trips, and from the road to the school is a half-mile. He worked all day long, walking back and forth until about six o'clock, when it was getting dark, and he was exhausted. So then after all that work, he had to hire a couple of men to complete the job. It almost killed him. Of course, he never asked us for help.

"Well, he set the desks up in his classroom. He moved the old desks to the side. The trouble was that the students came in early in the morning, about six o'clock, to study because they can't study in the villages. Of course, the students moved Bastone's desks around, because they're light and because they just did it. So when Bastone would come to teach, the desks would be all over the place. You know, they just wouldn't be in straight rows. And this was the problem. He wanted the desks in straight rows, but they weren't. Understand? Teachers are like that; they usually like straight rows.

"So Bastone asked Mr. Ngoma, the headmaster, for a key to lock the classroom. He wanted to keep it locked until he came in the morning. But Ngoma would not let him do this because he knew the students used the room to study in the morning. So they had an argument and Bastone lost. OK? To make it short, Bastone took all the desks back and he hired some guys to carry them up here, and he put all of them in his room.

"He stuffed all forty desks into his little room," I continued. "Actually, a few wouldn't fit, so he kept them here in the living room. You saw a couple of them here. Anyway, the room was like a cave. The desks went right up to the ceiling, one stacked on another. You couldn't get in the room. He made a little tunnel to walk to his bed between all the desks. Then he had another tunnel against the back wall to walk to his stove. It was ridiculous. The room was completely full. From floor to ceiling: desks, desks, desks. And he lived in this cave for months and months, until yesterday, when he moved them out and put them on the bus for somewhere. He's leaving in a few weeks, so he had to get rid of them, I guess." I let Lester digest this a little. "He's a crazy *mzungu* [a white person or European], isn't he? A good guy, but pretty flaky."

It was the type of story that makes no one laugh. It was too odd to be amusing. Lester simply looked around at us a few times but said nothing, and the rest of us said nothing either.

"Well, I'll be sad to see him go," Mike said, finally. "He's a real character, and I'll miss all his stunts. Anyway, he's real nice to bring the three kids home with him."

Our conversation drifted off into small talk. John explained what he was going to do on the upcoming Christmas school holiday, and we all agreed a vacation break was in order for the three cooks and for Paxton, too. We would work out the details later. We also agreed that we would buy the three boys some new clothes for their big trip. John and Robert and Lester excused themselves and drifted back to their house, and soon Mike set off for the hospital. I helped carry the dishes to the sink in the kitchen.

"So, what do you think about the boys going home with Bastone? It's pretty amazing he's going to take them," I said.

"Oh, yes, boss. This Bastone is a good man. Robert and Lester have been saying this to ourselves." Jordan began washing the dishes. "Boss," Jordan spoke and then hesitated.

"What, Jordan?"

"Do you, my boss, think you could take me home to Boston when you depart this next year? I can be your cook such as I am."

I hesitated a moment. "Oh, Jordan, I don't know. It's a tricky thing. It's difficult to imagine it, really." I stopped to gather my thoughts. "One problem is that people in the United States really don't have cooks. Only the really rich people can afford them. You think I am rich, and I can understand this, but I'm not. When I go home, I won't even have a job." I stopped again. It was a delicate issue, and I wanted to make myself clear and to explain what was so obvious to me. "People like me can afford servants only when we are here. The salaries of cooks and houseboys in Malawi are so low that we can do it. A cook in the United States would cost thousands of pounds per year. Cooks do not work cheaply. So only the very rich people have cooks. You see, almost everyone cooks for themselves. This is just the way it is."

"Is it? There can be no cooks to Boston?"

"Well, there's a few, but not many. People can't afford cooks. Really."

Jordan thought this over and then turned from the sink. "Is this to New York the same? These people you have spoken I take to be very rich indeed. Are they having cooks?"

"Nope. They're just like the people in Boston. No cooks. It's just that people like cars. I guess they like both cars and cooks. But they can't afford both." I hope I was being persuasive. "Besides, Jordan, you probably wouldn't like it in the States. It's not the same as here."

"Why is this, boss?"

"The people aren't Malawians. It's a different culture. No one speaks Chichewa, and the way of living is different. It's just a very different place. You might like it for a while, but you'd probably get lonely. You'd miss Ida and the kids and your village. Things like this."

"Are you lonely for your village to Boston, boss?"

"Sometimes. Yes, I get lonely, a little homesick. It's natural. I mean that's my home, and I'm used to it. I think people feel best where they come from. That's why I don't think you'd be happy there if you stayed for a long time."

Jordan continued to wash the last few cups. "Well, perhaps I could come to visit you to Boston."

"Now that's a good idea. If we could get the money together for a visit, then this would be good. You'd like it then. I could take you around and show you things. Maybe someday I'll be rich enough to send you the money for a plane ticket. Then we could have some fun."

Jordan seemed pleased with this idea and it seemed like a good idea to me too. We smiled at each other.

"Say, boss, why do you not stay to Malawi? This is a too good job you are having. I can be your cook for so many years to the future. Are you not liking this place?"

"Oh, Jordan, I like Malawi a lot. It's a great place. It's just that it's not home. The job, as you say, is good too, but I am just doing it for now. It's hard to explain. In six months I'll go home to do something else, to be with my family and my friends. I don't know why. It just seems like that's what I should do. And I do miss my home. I guess I just think I'll be happy there, like you are in Magola village."

"I am understanding, my boss. But I will be missing you then. For my whole life this can be."

"This could be, Jordan." I spoke quickly but realized suddenly I had not fully considered this sad prospect. After a year and a half in Malawi, I was becoming excited about going home, and it was a frequent topic of conversation among us. For us young men, the Peace Corps was a hiatus between college and a career, and while our service was a meaningful experience, it was not the basis on which we would build our careers. I knew I was reacting superficially. Working in the Peace Corps was not just something to do, something to be done with. Jordan was important to me, as were the others. He was a friend. Surely our friendship would not be over once I left. Relationships would go on, or at least they could go on in some way if people wanted them to. Our relationship did not have to end abruptly. I found myself wondering what would happen between us. "Look, Jordan, I can't say what will happen. I think we'll always be friends, don't you?"

"I am thinking this is true myself, boss."

I smiled and shook my head. "Tell me something. You've been a cook for lots of people over the years, and you've seen people come and go. I mean you work for someone for a few years. You get to know them. Then they leave. This is always happening. What do you feel about this? Do you get sad? I mean how do you feel about Dan and Bastone leaving?"

"This depends, my boss. This Dan is a bad man to me so it is good that he can go. The bwana Bastone, well he is a little bit crazy as you say. Well, he is not crazy this is true but he is too funny. Well, he is, what is this word to English, peculiar, and doing the crazy things all this time. But I take him to be a good man." Jordan paused for a few moments. "Well, he will go and what can I say. I cannot be seeing Bastone again. This I doubt. But this is the way of the life."

"So you miss some people, and others you don't care about. Right? I guess that sounds normal. I'm the same too."

"Well, we poor Africans, we must be doing these jobs for the work. We must be living, and so these azungu people are the bosses for us. It is the work that we must have. It is not the bosses."

"You mean the people don't matter. It's just the jobs and the money that's important?"

"It is a little bit like that. But it is different. The bosses can be good people and so we can be missing them. Some we take to be good bwanas so it is sad when they are departing. But we must have the jobs for our living. And we are just staying."

"Is someone like Bastone a friend? What's a friend?" I asked seriously.

"This Bastone is just someone to know. I have stated this. A friend can be different. It is more. The friend is helping and if we make the mistake it is still the friend. The friend can last and like the God can forgive the person and can help when there is the trouble."

"Do you think you'll miss Mike and me when we leave?" Perhaps it was an unfair question, but I had asked it before thinking.

"I cannot imagine, my bwana. This will be the too sad day of my life." Jordan swallowed deeply. It was egotistical and a little unfair on my part to have asked the question, but I was happy with the reply.

"Me too, Jordan. It will be a sad day. But I won't forget you. We'll always be friends. OK?"

"OK, my boss."

Chapter Ten

Some Joy Too

I stepped carefully on the stones that filled the small stream along the lower edge of the hospital property. Large trees enjoyed the year-round water supply, and the area was shady, almost dark. I was taking a shortcut back from Gumbu village, where I had been seeing a patient. Dr. Johnson, our new physician, had asked me to assist him in the theatre at three o'clock. I caught sight of Mike as I stepped from the thick bushes and made my way up the steep slope. He stood before the unfinished tuberculosis ward, which had recently been fitted with a new roof. Our friend Makwangwala had organized the building of this badly needed addition to our crowded little hospital, and it now seemed it would be finished before we would leave for home. Mike had taken considerable interest in the project and was in the process of ordering beds, mattresses, and tables to get it properly equipped. I stopped to speak to him, and he outlined what he had in mind. The new ward was far from fancy, but it had good ventilation, and we would be able to separate our highly contagious patients from the others.

"It's coming along pretty well. I'd say in a month we could use it, if we get the furniture," Mike said.

"What did USAID [United States Agency for International Development] say? Did you call them this morning?"

"They said OK. They'll get Medical Supplies to send the stuff up, and they'll reorder new beds and things to replenish the stores. They see no problem. So I guess it'll work."

Mike took me into the building to show me what the laborers were doing. He enjoyed seeing the building coming to completion. In a job like ours it was difficult to measure success, since most of the

113

patients did not dramatically recover. Much of our work was spent on collecting statistics to profile the health conditions of the people, so I often asked myself if I was doing any good at all. Over the months, I had become hardened to the suffering I saw daily in the hospital, and I was bothered by how callous I had become. I realized that the health conditions in Malawi were insurmountable: no real improvements were possible. Although poor nutrition and bad water were major problems, it was poverty and the government's political decision not to give health a high priority that prevented even manageable diseases like polio or smallpox from receiving attention. Many health problems could be solved or improved upon fairly cheaply if money and a little expertise were available, but this was not the situation here, and I saw little likelihood for change. A building like this was at least something you could see and touch. It was a little sign of progress and would ease the suffering of a few. Or so I hoped.

"Say, I just heard some bad news," Mike spoke.

"Now what?" My voice trembled.

"Chumia's daughter died yesterday. Sunday," Mike continued.

"Chumia's daughter died? Which one? You mean the cute little one about three years old? I saw her just a few days ago. I can't believe it." Phil Chumia was the number two man at the hospital. Like Misomali, he was a medical assistant and a very capable man. Dr. Johnson, who had recently come to replace Misomali, thought a lot of Chumia, and the two of them worked well together. Chumia had received some national attention several years before, when he was the chief health assistant at a small clinic twenty miles south of Ntcheu at a place called Balaka. A crazed hyena had entered a village late at night and had attacked a woman as she was walking back to her house after using the latrine. Her screams woke other villagers, who came to her assistance, only to be victimized by the hyena. One by one people were attacked and ripped apart. Large chunks of flesh, Chumia had explained, were brutally severed from their legs and backs. It was a hellish experience. Before the hyena ran off, it claimed twenty-three victims, including one infant, whom it carried off and presumably ate. The savaged victims were carried to the clinic, and Chumia had miraculously saved all but seven of them. The government had publicly cited him for his ability in the disaster and although he passed it off as simply doing his duty, he did show me a photograph of the hyena after it was eventually shot and carried, slung under a long pole, into the local police station. Chumia seemed a happy man, and he drank beer with us from time to time, and we considered him a good friend. "How did she die?" I asked Mike.

"Malaria. Can you believe it? She died of malaria," Mike answered.

"You've got to be kidding. How could she die of malaria? He could have easily treated her." My response was aggressive. So little could be done for many diseases, but malaria was one thing that could normally be treated. This should not have happened.

Mike waited a moment, as if to let me grasp the full impact of the news. "Well, the tragedy is that he had no malaria drugs." He paused. "He didn't have any pills."

"Come on, Mike. The hospital's full of pills. There must be boxes of them. That's one thing we have."

"We ran out last week, maybe a few weeks ago. They just ordered some more. You know how the ordering goes: don't order until you're completely out; then you know for sure you need it. It's sad, man." Mike waited some more as I looked out into space and tried to comprehend this senseless tragedy. He continued, "She got sick on Friday and was really bad on Saturday. He didn't do anything for a while because, you know, sometimes they like the kids to go through malaria once to sort of build up an immunity to it, or so they say. Anyway, on Saturday night he realized she was real bad, and he went over to the stores to get some malaria pills. And, there weren't any."

"Goddamn it, why didn't he just come over to our house? We've got thousands of damn pills between us." I spoke with disbelief and frustration and anger. My question required no answer, and Mike knew it. Chumia likely felt that in spite of the severity of the illness, she would pull through, as most children did. The pills would help, but they were not critical. They would shorten the duration of the illness, but she would recover without them. And, Chumia knew that medicines were imperfect and sometimes had negative side effects. But still, why did he not come to us? Did we appear incapable of understanding his choices and were thus unapproachable? I had difficulty in trying to comprehend this, sorting it out. Death and indescribable suffering were commonplace in our little hospital, and it was easy to become callous when you worked around it as we did every day. This child I knew and the situation was not abstract—it was personal and painful. Like so many things here, I would deal with it in some fashion, but for now I would just have to carry my grief and my anger.

Mike and I said nothing more to each other as we walked up the hill to the hospital. Mike turned toward the tiny laboratory, and I continued on to the theatre.

Dr. Johnson—Anthony, as we called him—was an Englishman about thirty years of age. He had come to Ntcheu four months before with his Indian wife, and Misomali had stayed on for some three months to assist him in making the transition to practice in this most difficult place. Now Anthony was on his own, and things were not going well. Anthony's skills as a physician may have been considerable, but he was poorly equipped for working here where administrative abilities and new approaches to problems were required, where different outlooks and attitudes were essential. With no surgical training to speak of, he was particularly vulnerable, and poor Anthony was proving to be a miserable failure in the area of surgery. To compound the problems, Anthony was a poor observer of the world around him. His fine education had taught him to think abstractly, but his job here required him to work concretely, to grasp clearly the real world of events, to know what was going on around him. Recently, he had assigned to Mr. Nyirenda, the senior clerk, a house that had become vacant on the hospital property. This decision had become a major source of discontent among the senior medical staff, whose status was far higher than Nyirenda's, and I was beginning to get hints that some staff members were starting to take political action against him via the local political party. To add to his troubles, he often made snap judgments about complex issues that required careful analysis, and frequently they were poor judgments, which inevitably had to be reversed.

Despite his shortcomings, we liked Anthony. He was generous and kind and legitimately cared for the people. His willingness to accept a rural posting such as this was admirable, since it was a poor place to practice medicine and successes would be few. It took a special person, psychologically and physically strong, to make it; and while a final judgment on Anthony would wait, his willingness to put himself in this difficult position was laudable. Evidently, Anthony came from a well-to-do family and was a man of some refinement and taste; while he contrasted quite dramatically from all of us, his pleasant demeanor—informal, sincere, never arrogant, and rarely judgmental—bridged any differences of age or background that may have existed. I caught up with him in the little anteroom of the surgical theatre. Remarkably, Chumia, who would assist Anthony as the anesthesiologist, was with him, and I was struck by the strength of this man who could function in spite of his own personal grief. To Chumia I expressed my sincere condolence and then turned to Anthony.

"What's up, Anthony? You said this is an appendicitis case." I began to put on a sterile gown so that I could be of some use to them during the operation. It was essential that we take all the necessary steps to prevent infection, although nothing ever seemed really sterilized to me. Our large autoclaves were heated by simple kerosene stoves that could not produce the high temperatures or the high pressures required. The gowns and cloth drapes appeared soiled; the metal instruments I could only speculate about. I knew that most operations failed, even if performed well, because of infection; operations were a last resort, an act of desperation.

"It's an old woman. She's got all the symptoms, so I've got to operate." Anthony finished scrubbing his hands. Chumia was in the theatre preparing the sodium pentothal. "Here she comes now." He nodded to a poor old lady who slowly and painfully walked with the aid of a medical assistant through our dingy scrub room to the theatre and to the operating table. It was a remarkable sight.

I finished dressing. My gown, mask, and cap were simply placed over my regular clothes, the ones I had worn all afternoon in the village, my shoes having stepped on any manner of filth. I looked into the theatre to see this poor creature stripped of all her clothing, and then with a little help she pulled her skinny body up on the table. Her eyes displayed a fear I had never seen before in anyone. She was terrified. Someone facing a firing squad perhaps had a face in such anguish, and she may well have analyzed her upcoming ordeal similarly. But unlike the firing squad victim, she seemed confused, and I wondered if she knew what was to happen or even, beyond some general notion, why she was here. This added a pathetic quality to the event. To subject this human being to the acts of others without full comprehension was a denial of her humanity, and her face seemed to beg for understanding even as she was pushed and prodded by the well-meaning attendants.

I entered the theatre and stood across from Anthony. A medical assistant was at his side, poised to hand him instruments. Chumia was stationed by her head, and the tubes to carry the sodium pentothal were already in her arm. She was fully draped, with only the lower right quadrant of her abdomen exposed. We were ready, our masks and caps were in place, and Chumia stepped forward and placed the blood pressure cuff and stethoscope on her left arm. He asked me to hold the syringe containing the powerful sedative, and I took it from a small table and stood by his side.

"Say, Anthony, are you sure she really has appendicitis?" It was a bold question to ask at this late moment.

"Of course. What do you mean?" Anthony looked at me from under his mask.

I hesitated a moment. "Well, are we sure this is the problem?" My question challenged his decision, but I hoped it would be regarded as simply one final and legitimate check. "I mean I've never heard of old people like this having their appendix out. Couldn't it be something else? Maybe a drug reaction to something or even a translation problem. I mean, who did the translation for you when you examined her?''

Anthony looked at me. His ability as a diagnostician was severely hampered because our lab was so poor and because his ability to communicate with patients, always through translators, was minimal. Furthermore, he was incapable of understanding the translator's lack of sophistication in medicine or his limited capacity with English or the status relationships between him as a white European physician and them as junior Malawian workers. I could imagine Anthony asking complex questions that were never understood by the translator—and certainly not by the patient— and then receiving answers completely unrelated to the question and consequently dangerous if accepted without skepticism.

"OK, that's all for now. The surgery is postponed." He reached down and touched the woman's leg. "It's OK, madam. We're not going to operate today. You can go back to your room for now." He pulled down his mask and began taking off his surgical gloves, and he walked from the theatre.

Chumia spoke to the poor lady, who was no doubt more confused than ever. The medical assistant began to put the instruments away, and I handed Chumia his syringe and joined Anthony in the anteroom.

"Maybe she doesn't have appendicitis. We'll wait and see." Anthony spoke matter-of-factly as he took off his gown. I said nothing, trying to hide my disbelief at his calling off the procedure after one simple and uninformed question. If he was embarrassed by his quick reversal, he did not show it, and I admired him in an odd way for being able to change his mind.

"You look to be very upset, my bwana," Jordan spoke, his voice was serious, displaying his concern. I had stopped by his room to play with his little daughter Mari, as I frequently did in the late afternoon. I sat on a large log that the woodman had recently delivered and was trying to have a game of catch with an old tennis ball I had given her.

"Oh, I'm OK, Jordan," I replied. My voice must have indicated something very different, though.

"Sure, boss? You seem to be a little bit unhappy this day. This I can see."

"Well, it's just a sad day, that's all." I hesitated. "Like a lot of days around here."

"Is this so? This is a sad day? Why is that?"

I did not reply at first. Playing with Mari was all I wished to do. It was simple, and she seemed to enjoy it, and I needed things to be simple for a while. He waited for a reply. "Things are so screwed up all the time. Nothing works. People die all over the place, all the time, for no reason. The whole damn country's a shambles, a total goddamned pathetic mess. Nothing works right. People suffer all over the place. It's hopeless. Nothing's happening. Nothing works except suffering. It's a ridiculous, pathetic, screwed-up mess, and it's never going to get any better. Never. It's a place of pain, that's all. Pure and simple."

"This cannot be, my boss. The things can be just the same as they are. The lives of the people it is difficult this is true, but we can be enjoying too. We have the lives to live and so we must be living. It is the gift we have to live and to enjoy the good of our lives."

I paused. "Jordan, I know what you're saying about life itself, but I'm really asking the other part of the question. Why is there so much suffering here? And I don't see how it's going to change. There's no real chance to improve things. People are just doomed to suffer, and I mean suffer horribly." I waited a few moments. "Look, I don't mean that being poor is necessarily bad. Living in the villages can be enjoyable or even good, I suppose. I mean pain. Kids dying and people starving, and stupid diseases which you can cure, but not here. Things like no operations for the simplest things. Just look around at all the cripples you see. Guys crawling around on their knees and begging all over the place. This is what I mean." Jordan just looked at me. He apparently knew I needed to speak. "That hospital over there is a cesspool, a goddamn joke. It's not a hospital. It's a death factory to stick people in and let them suffer." My voice became louder and I was becoming more enraged. "Did you hear that Chumia's daughter died yesterday?"

"No, my boss. I did not know. This is a too sad thing you are telling me." Jordan's voice was soft.

"You bet your ass, it's sad. And you know why? Because there were no goddamn malaria pills in a country full of malaria. The simplest and most common drug in the country, and we don't have any. And if you need an operation, you can't get one, and if you got one, they'd screw it up somehow, and then you'd die of infection anyway. There's no health system here. It's a goddamn farce. You're better off going to the witch doctor for a little ju-ju medicine. At least he wouldn't cut off your wrong damn leg or something, or take your appendix out when it was OK."

We both remained silent for a few minutes, and I resumed my game with little Mari, who had stopped to watch me sound off so bitterly. Jordan finally spoke, "This I can see is a sad day for my boss. Yes, I can see this to be so."

I took a deep breath. I began to speak softly and with some control. "Jordan, I'm sorry, and this sounds terrible, but all the days here are sad ones. Today's no different. It's just that I know Chumia, and so it's a personal thing today. But it's no different than another day. See what I mean?''

Jordan thought for a moment. "It is just a bit I am seeing. But this I do not take to be true. There is not just the sadness as you are speaking. There is the good too.''

"Come on, Jordan. What good is there? The schools stink, and hardly anyone gets into them anyway. There's hardly any old people in the villages. People work themselves to death and starve half the time. They don't have anything. They wear ragged old clothes, and half of them look sick all the time. The beggars and cripples are everywhere. Now tell me this doesn't make things sad. Tell me.''

"These things you mention can be so, my boss. Some of these things are too terrible indeed. This I know to be true. But there is the good and the people can be so happy. True. I am knowing this.''

"The people must be pretty stupid then to go through all this and still be happy." My remark was thoughtless, unkind, and uncalled for; quickly I began to apologize. "Jordan, that was a stupid thing for me to say. I'm sorry I said it. My point is that I just don't understand. How can people think there's any good here? How can they be happy with everything so bad? Can you explain that to me? I'd like to know. Please tell me how they can be happy.''

Jordan stared at me. His face was serious and yet slightly flushed, as if he were embarrassed. I needed his help, an explanation of some sort, and I knew that he, a friend, would try. He looked up at the sky and then down at little Mari and then back to me. This was a challenging request, and he struggled to get his thoughts together.

"The bwanas can have so many things, the money and the clothes and the cars and all the good such as this that we poor African people do not have. This I can see." He paused, "I do not know why the God has made this to be so but this is the way of the world. And so I must accept. What can I do? I am poor. I have so few things as you, my bwana, know. But, boss, I am a happy chap and this I can say is true." He waited a moment. "As for the people, many can be too poor. They have less than I, Jordan, for I am a cook. But they can be happy. I take them to be so." He stopped and waited a moment, perhaps to see if I believed him.

"All right, Jordan, I've got you. You're happy and I take your word for it, and I guess the village people are happy in some sort of a way too. But the question to me is still why? Why are they happy? It still seems there's so much to be unhappy about that outweighs the good parts of their lives.''

"Well, boss, the people can work so hard to have the life. True, it is very difficult." He thought for a moment. "But the life is more than the money and the clothes. My bwanas have these things but there is more for the bwanas as it is so to the people. We can have the beautiful children and the laughing and we have this nature to see. We can make the party for dancing and for eating. We have so many friends and the families for loving them and for the marriage to love the wife. And, boss, we can have the wish for the better life for the family and this is the wishing which is good, too. We have this, I know this to be true for I wish for my children to be better than such as I, Jordan. My mind is seeing this to the imagination." He paused. "The sadness is in the life such as to be sick and to die but this is to the life of the bwanas, too. I take our lives to be so much the same for the children are born and we are raising them and schooling them such as you. We have so many happy days to the marriages and the births and the celebration to puberty, and for the success of the children. And for myself as when the crop is good and when I have the nice clothes and when we are having the beer parties to the village, as with my bwanas. So the life is the life. It can be good and with the joy. The poverty can be the most big problem but the things of the life are too many and so the poorness is just one thing of it. And so, we have the days of our happiness, as the bwanas can be happy, without the money." He stopped talking and looked at me. "Are you understanding me what I have spoken, boss?"

I stood for several moments and simply stared into space. "Yeah, I do. I understand, Jordan. And I should have known already what you just said. I feel stupid. Of course, the people have happiness and some hope too." We both sat down for a few minutes and I finished my game. I turned to Jordan. "Say, achimwene, your explanation was a good one, and I thank you for it. I do think people's lives can have joy in them and that people can be happy, even if things are very difficult at times. I'll look more carefully at their faces when I'm in the villages to see if it's there like you say." I waited a moment more before standing. "I'm going to take a nap. I'll see you at dinner. And, Jordan, thanks. I feel a lot better than a few minutes ago. Ndapita."

"Zikomo, my bwana."

Chapter Eleven

Playing With Prejudice

The Kandoto Markets were Malawi's largest chain of grocery stores, and these were part of a parent company that had been in Nyasaland throughout the colonial period and had had various types of holdings in farming, in importing and exporting, or in retailing, depending on the exigencies of a given time. Always profitable, they continued to operate, presumably still with profits, in this new era of independence.

The Blantyre store was the country's largest; and while it had some of the appearances of a modern supermarket, it had limited offerings, and most of these were imported and expensive. The European community and Malawian elites were the only customers. The lower-echelon civil servants and the other lower-wage laborers of the city preferred to use the open African market.

Saturday mornings were busy days in town as people from farms, missions, rural hospitals, and outlying development projects came to shop. The central business district of Blantyre was small, with three tiny blocks and an adjoining road of Indian shops that stretched for about a quarter-mile. The crowds were small, but there was an air of festivity as people scurried about to do their banking or marketing before the town shut down at noon.

I joined Jordan and Mike at Kandoto. The European madams, as Jordan called them, strolled through the aisles to gather whatever suited them. Some were joined by their cooks, and some had young boys in tow, hired to carry the baskets for the madams. The three of us were a rag tag outfit by comparison, since the issue of money was something we took seriously, unlike the madams who bought and bought, oblivious to cost. It was true that living in Ntcheu was inexpensive; in fact, there was nothing to spend your money on except food and cigarettes and beer. In Blantyre, things were different. Supermarkets like this offered temptations in bottled and canned goods unknown in the rural areas. Our small salaries forced us to make careful choices of what we bought and our shopping sprees in the big city required thought and some restraint. The fact that Jordan had come to Blantyre with us this weekend and that he saw no limits to our abilities to spend complicated our trip to the market more than usual.

Peanut butter and jams were essential for us, as were curries and chutneys and other sauces to flavor our bland food at home, and Jordan and Mike had nearly filled a small basket with these items. We could have bought more, but things were heavy; and our trip home, requiring many miles of walking just to get to the bus station or to the main road north where we could hitchhike, would become unnecessarily burdened.

Jordan loved to shop like this. A cook needed supplies to be creative, and the more we could buy, the better. Mike, I guessed, had to turn him down on many requests, but there were enough tins and jars to last us for a month or more. I joined them as they strolled down the final aisle and after some discussion we added to our basket three boxes of spaghetti and two large bottles of ketchup, an important seasoning for both beef and goat.

"Hey, Jordan, look at the woman over there. See how much stuff she's buying?" Jordan and Mike glanced down the aisle toward a white woman in her late forties. She was standing beside a cart stuffed with boxes of cereal and little tins of smelts and bars of chocolate and bottles of Scotch whisky and dozens of other expensive little treasures.

In addition, she had purchased her meat and bread and even her vegetables here, items that we would purchase in the market or from boys on the street at considerably lower prices. Money seemed to be of little concern to her, and the scale of her purchases seemed inappropriately large and contrasted harshly and offensively with the poverty and the scarcity of material goods that was so obvious in the lives of the locals.

"It would be fun to buy all that, wouldn't it, Jordan? Then we could put it into our Land Rover and drive back to Ntcheu. And maybe we could stop up on the Shire River and have a picnic and drink all the whiskey. That would be neat, wouldn't it?" I tried my little fantasy out on Jordan.

He looked at me seriously but missed my cynical tone. "Oh, that would be jolly good, my boss. But these items she has purchased are very dear and my bosses are not having the money such as this. This I know."

"Well, why do you think this woman's got all this money and we don't? Why do you think white people, except for us, have money and the Africans are poor?"

"I am not knowing this my boss. It is the way. This I can see, but I am not knowing," Jordan answered.

"Well, why don't we go up and ask this lady why she's rich? Maybe she has a secret that she can tell us. Maybe she has a machine that makes money, or maybe a gold mine in South Africa. What do you think?"

Mike smiled and Jordan, after carefully listening to me, eventually smiled too. The three of us walked on to the check-out area and stood behind our lady friend, who was busy emptying her cart.

"You know, Jordan, this lady drinks one of those bottles of whiskey every day." I spoke just loudly enough for the woman to hear me. Mike smiled and began to chuckle. Jordan registered little expression. He was uncomfortable with my wisecrack, presumably seeing no reason to harass the woman and certainly not wanting to be involved in some sort of verbal skirmish with a European. I continued, "It's true. All the European women drink a bottle of whiskey every day and most of them have ten bottles of beer besides that. Isn't that true, Mike?"

"Sure is. And they drink wine with every meal, including breakfast, and have gin and tonics steadily from four to six o'clock every afternoon, and then they start drinking whiskey again. And this lasts all night, except during their dinner, when they drink wine."

Jordan stared at us. "You didn't know this, Jordan? We thought you knew this was how the madams passed the time. I mean, how else could they get through the day? They don't do anything except play golf and tennis and bridge and shop for more whiskey and wine. So the madams are a little drunk all day long. Really, it's true," I continued, but Jordan was becoming visibly uneasy with our nasty remarks, and although we might have continued with a more receptive audience, he clearly wanted us to stop. The face of our lady friend gave every indication of being offended too, and so we stopped while she finished at the check-out line. Our relationship with the expatriate British community had been a confusing one at times. They were the great exploiters, knowingly or not, and we of course were the great saviors, picking up the pieces of the shattered empire. New secondary-school openings since independence meant a huge teacher shortage, and Peace Corps teachers now comprised nearly 70 percent of these teachers. Why had the British not done more? Why had the expatriates, who lived most comfortably, not given more? Questions such as these were frequently on our minds; and while the answers were complex and historical in nature, they were still very much a real issue. The expatriates were still here, making profits and living well, and they would not be leading any change to a more just society.

Their lifestyles and ours, oriented as we were to the rural areas and to lower positions of government, were sufficiently different that we had little contact with the expatriate community. True, our occasional meetings sometimes produced strident clashes, but the basis of our antagonism was imperfectly understood by us. These people lived a good life, certainly a better one than they would have had at home, and the quality of their fine lives was based on a system that expropriated wealth from the Malawian peasants. This much seemed perfectly clear. On the other hand, these people, like the Malawians themselves, were products of the system of colonialism and were shaped by its structure even as they in turn shaped it. While it was easy to understand how they were in imperfect control of their circumstances, we still found their attitudes toward Malawians to be outrageous at times. Their positions of privilege needed to be rationalized. And the notion that Malawians were inferiors who needed the expatriates and the expatriates' institutions was an essential ingredient in this rationalization. As volunteers, we held generally different assumptions about Malawians, even if at times they were a bit naive. And our sense of the supposed contribution of the British to Malawian history was something we remained skeptical about. Surely Malawi would have developed on its own, as most places did, if the British had not been present. It was anyone's guess whether the lives of the Malawians would have been better or worse, but it was difficult to imagine much worse.

Yet the situation was more complex. The expatriate community was not monolithic. Many were sympathetic and kind and wished the Malawians well. Many had recently arrived to assist in the transition to nationhood and were offering their talents generously, even if for money. Many had been staunch supporters of independence, and many, even some of the old-timers, were abandoning their long-held outlooks and were entering into new social relationships, with newly changing attitudes. Our harsh remarks did not take into account the type of person this woman was and, of course, we had been unfair. Additionally, we ended up making Jordan miserable as we stereotyped her and therefore all the British—one of the very things we accused them of doing to the Malawians.

On an individual level, the antagonism between volunteers and the British seemed to be forgotten. While they regarded us as a little peculiar, volunteering to do what any sensible person would do for money, they judged us as individuals, and friendships were formed on the basis of personal likes and dislikes. My impression was that we all had expatriate friends, either long-term colonials or recent arrivals on contract, and these expatriates were an interesting group of people to become acquainted with, and we benefited from the relationships.

The seedy El Brazil Coffee Shop, located on a little side street, was our next stop. It was a Saturday morning hangout for Peace Corps volunteers when they came to town, and this day the four inside booths and three tables on the khonde were filled, while additional customers stood waiting for a seat. The number of volunteers in Malawi had grown to over 250; many lived in such isolated areas that it was difficult for them to travel, yet the numbers were sufficiently large that some thirty or forty volunteers were in town on any given Saturday.

Mike and I were to play rugby at four o'clock at the Blantyre sports club when things had cooled off a little. We played for a team comprised entirely of Americans and, showing little imagination and a little nationalism, we called ourselves the Yanks. Our team became the fifth one in the rugby league, and since we had no home pitch, we played all our games at one of the established sports clubs. As beginners, we had been most unsuccessful. We had, in fact, lost all our games, and in spite of having a handful of athletes who had the skills for a rough game like rugby, we generally offered the opposition little real competition. Nevertheless, Mike and I loved the game and the camaraderie that provided so welcome a change from our lives as health workers.

In addition to Mike and me, John Devendorff, Doug Smith, and Bill Kinsel, who had recently moved to Ntcheu, also played; so when we came down on weekends, we would rent a small car to get around in. Generally, we rented it on Friday afternoon and returned it on Sunday morning, when we began our arduous trip home. With five people renting the car, we kept it in constant motion throughout the weekend, and generally we simply disconnected the odometer and returned it with only a fraction of the real mileage recorded. Our larceny we excused away some way or other, and we took delight in outsmarting the English businessmen who managed the garage for a large multinational corporation.

As we approached the coffee shop, we came to our car. There we locked our purchases in the trunk and joined our friends.

Jordan seemed to feel a little awkward at first, but by the time we finally got a seat on the khonde he was reasonably relaxed. Other volunteers, learning he was our cook, went out of their way to talk to him; and Jordan, the skillful conversationalist, engaged them easily in small talk. Very few cooks in similar positions would be comfortable sitting here, but Jordan had a certain pride, a certain confidence in himself, that enabled him to mix with others of so-called higher standing. Jordan knew he was intelligent, but more importantly he could explain with some clarity and personal satisfaction why he, bright and ambitious, was deficient in the credentials that would allow him any real social mobility. On several occasions, he had explained to me about the inability of his parents to afford his school fees and how that had eventually blocked his path. Simple villagers rarely got ahead, he explained. Those who would complete school were the children of civil servants or others who were at least engaged in some form of wage employment. Simply put, the privileged within Malawian society, and naturally the privileged within society during the colonial period, were able to pass on these advantages to their own children: common villagers, like Jordan, were effectively excluded.

Jordan's understanding of social mobility was crucial to explaining his own life. He seemed to grasp the idea that one's position had been shaped by social forces, blocking some and pulling others, and that the social structure or people's positions within it was the major determinant of one's mobility or lack of it. This insight, it seemed, was the basis on which he assessed himself, the basis of his confidence and pride in himself. He lacked opportunity, not ability.

The Safari Restaurant, our next stop, was a fancy place with twenty or more tables covered with clean white tablecloths, and with waiters who were skilled and wore neat uniform jackets to complete the effect. The bar area was large, too, and on this Saturday morning it was crowded, even before noon. We were to meet with several teammates for lunch and to get organized for our game later in the afternoon. We would be together for a long time, maybe as late as four or five o'clock the following morning, when the post-game rugby shenanigans finally ended. In this expatriate society, with lots of men and few single European women, a great deal of drinking was done, and a Saturday night rugby party was the perfect setting. We would skip the beer now, the demands of the strenuous game ahead dictating some sensible behavior.

By one o'clock we were through eating, and we decided to return to the large hostel that the Peace Corps rented for our visits to town. We would rest a few hours before heading over to the Blantyre Sports Club. As we sorted out our checks, I spoke quietly to Jordan. "Say, achimwene, we're going back to the hostel for a while before our game, so I guess we won't see you until tomorrow."

"Why is this, my boss?" Jordan seemed a little confused.

"Well, because our game won't be over much before six o'clock, and then we'll be drinking beer most of the night, and tomorrow we won't get up until about noon. And since there are so many of us, we've decided not to hitchhike home. We'll take the night bus back to Ntcheu. It'll be horrible, but it's the only way we can do it. OK?" I explained our plans while Jordan nodded. "Tomorrow we'll meet you at Maxim's restaurant at five o'clock, and after we eat, we can walk over to the bus. It's only about a mile or so." I reached into my pocket and passed him a one pound note. "Take this for food until we meet tomorrow. Buy your friend in Ndirande some beer too, OK?" Our plan was simple, and we were sure Jordan would have no objection.

Jordan took the note and looked across the room, saying nothing. Finally, he turned to Bill Kinsel and John and me, who were at the end of the table near him. "But, my bwanas, can I not come to this athletic contest of which my bosses can be participating?"

The three of us stared at him momentarily and then at each other. Bill spoke, "What the hell do you want to do that for? It's just a bunch of crazy Englishmen and a few of us idiots in shorts beating each other and chasing a ball around. It's really stupid, believe me."

"But I did not see this contest of which my bwanas to Ntcheu are running each day to our house to become very fit. I am just wishing to see this." Jordan's request was reasonable. He had seen the five of us work out on a regular basis and he wanted to see how the game was played.

Bill's assertion that the game was silly and not worth seeing was well meant, but it failed to satisfy Jordan. The three of us squirmed a little, and, as Jordan waited patiently for a better answer, we became more uncomfortable. Our teammates at the table soon picked up on us, and I heard one of them whisper, "He wants to know why he can't come to the game today." Now everyone at the table was experiencing the same discomfort; and Jordan, aware that his sensitive question had placed him at the center of the issue, seemed somewhat embarrassed, too.

"Well, you know how these clubs are, Jordan. Only members can come, and these members are people who pay money to join," Mike explained.

"I am understanding this. I can know that this place is for the bwanas who are the Europeans." Jordan paused. "But can it be possible for a small chap such as Jordan to come to watch? I can just be sitting quietly to watch my bwanas."

It was a simple request, certainly one which did not deserve an unpleasant response. Mike, however, continued, "Jordan, the only members of the club are Europeans; all the workers are Malawians. I suppose rich Malawians could join, if they wished, now that Malawi has independence. But at this time, none want to join. Why would they want to, when you think about it? Most of the Europeans probably wouldn't be very nice to them, and also most of the Malawians wouldn't have enough money. Also, these British people really like clubs. It seems to be part of their life. They like sports, and they like pubs, and these clubs have both. So it's just the way they live.''

Mike's explanation was reasonable. The Europeans and the Africans had separate spheres of activity in certain areas of their lives, in this case in the area of recreation, and nothing should be inferred from this. It was true that the Europeans had more money, but Africans with money and the interest could become club members. Jordan thought carefully, and we watched him assess the explanation, knowing its shortcomings and, ultimately, our own shortcomings.

"Are you a member to this place, Michael?" Jordan asked.

"No, none of us is a member, so we can't sign you in. We're guests, too," Mike said.

"But there can be the others who are eating just here who cannot be the players and they can come to watch. Is this not so?" Jordan's assessment spoke right to the heart of the issue and exposed Mike's gentle but inadequate explanation.

"Jordan, they don't want Africans there. That's the end of the story," I said bluntly. Jordan already knew the real answer; it was silly to keep playing games with him. "And my guess is that they don't want any Africans, rich or poor, but of course they'd never admit that. Got it?"

"This is what I am thinking, my boss. This I take to be true. I cannot come to watch the contest because I am an African."

"That's what it amounts to. It's really amazing to have an independent African country with all European clubs. It's stupid, I know, but the whites still have all the money and the government wants them to stay here. So they have their clubs." My explanation shifted from Jordan to a broader explanation in an attempt to depersonalize the rejection. "Maybe we can talk about it some more on the bus tomorrow night, OK?" The others around the table seemed relieved that the conversation was ending, and they quickly began passing money to cover the bill.

Jordan watched as the money and the tip were placed in the center of the long table. Softly, he spoke to Mike and Bill and me as the others began to stand up, "Why can you, my good bwanas, that have been so good to us Africans, go to such a place?"

The three of us looked directly at each other, frozen. Jordan finally forced the conversation to a place where we could not escape. We were complicit.

"You little son of a bitch, Jordan, kicking us right in the balls.

Man, you're really making our life tough." I had no good explanation, and despite my playful counterattack, I recognized the poignancy and fairness of his question.

"Because we're racists, and we just like to be around white people. That's why we go there. And we have a secret altar in there, and we pray to the spirit of David Livingston, who made this all possible," Mike expanded upon my comments, and I forced a smile. Jordan simply stared; because we could give him no good answer, I guessed he felt, correctly, that there was none.

Our friends had reached the door but the four of us had remained sitting. "Look, Jordan, it's difficult for us to explain why we're going to play rugby in a club that basically allows only whites. We do not agree with the practice." I spoke without knowing what conclusion I would reach. "We feel very awkward, but we can't do much about it. And it's not going to change much now, whether we play or not. This isn't a good explanation, and I know it, so can we talk about it tomorrow on the bus?" My reply was pathetic but at least I had another day before I had to come face to face with Jordan.

"OK, my boss, this we can do, if you say." His face remained serious. He was looking for an explanation, it seemed, not simply trying to expose the inconsistency in our behavior.

The four of us quickly joined our friends at the door. Outside, Jordan left us for his friend's house in the shanty-town of Ndirande, and Mike explained our conversation to the others as we walked toward the hostel.

As expected, the ride on the night bus turned out to be a horror. We managed to get five seats in the front of the bus, directly alongside the driver and the engine covering. The door of the bus was in the middle; a conductor and bus manager collected tickets, and the driver simply drove. As usual, the bus was filled well beyond capacity, and the aisles were crammed with people, baskets, and chickens. Since it was difficult for passengers to make their way to the exit door, the luggage for departing passengers was generally passed along over the heads of the seated passengers. We were fortunate to have seats, especially together, and the fact that we were in the front allowed us a little privacy to talk, and to drink the beer which we had brought along. It would be a difficult six-hour ride. The bus would stop frequently to let passengers off or to allow groups of people, including us beer drinkers, to urinate along the side of the road. The bus went slowly and often shook violently as it pounded on the corrugations; sleeping, even resting, was impossible. We hated traveling this way and were generally depressed as we set off, knowing how boring and uncomfortable our journey would be.

We made a partial adaptation to the rhythm of the bus, and so we began to drink our beer and attempted to talk over the engine's loud roar. We talked about the game. We lost again, although there were a few stretches when we played respectably. Had we not had to play short handed with two players injured, we might have been in the entire game. We went on and on about various plays, like athletes anywhere, and Jordan soon lost interest in trying to make sense of it all.

"Why is it my bwanas are losing? I take you to be very big chaps and too fit," Jordan spoke.

We all smiled, and finally John spoke. "You're right there. We're all great athletes. It's just that we don't know what the hell we're doing. It's a small thing, not knowing how to play, but I'm sure we'll get the knack of it in a few years." We all laughed and looked to Jordan to see if he understood. He indicated nothing, and none of us bothered to explain further. We rode on.

"My bwanas," Jordan eventually spoke.

"Yes, Jordan," John answered.

"You are telling me to the restaurant that we will be talking to the bus this night. It is of this, I wish for you my bwanas to speak." Jordan was calling for the explanation. Secretly, we had all wished he would have forgotten it. We looked at one other to see who would speak. Since I had been with Jordan the longest and was closest to him, I seemed to be nominated.

"Well, achimwene, I don't know if I have a very good explanation for you," I started apologetically, promising little. "I think you know that we all like Malawians and wish the people here and the whole country well. But the question you're asking has to do with race relations, European and African relationships, and that is very complicated." I stopped to see if he was following me. "Now what is it you want to know?"

He spoke quickly. He was ready. "I can be wondering why the Europeans can have all the money and why they are treating us Africans such as they do. I should say not all the Europeans."

"Fair enough, Jordan. And also you want to know why we go to their clubs and hang around with them, right?" He did not reply to my question, but I knew this was part of the job before me. "Look, I don't know the whole story, but Europeans have money and farms and businesses because about four or five hundred years ago people in Europe began to develop a system of business called capitalism which meant that people for the first time wanted to make lots of money or profits. To do this, they needed the materials and cheap labor of other countries, so they sent out explorers and others to conquer places. In other words, the wealth of Europe comes about in part because the money of the Africans gets moved from Africa to Europe. So for Europe to be rich, Africa is poor.'' My explanation was abstract and ridiculously brief. It was a debate for historians who would either see benefit for Africans in their contact with Europeans or, as was fashionable, see harm in colonialism and neocolonialism. ''In other words, Europeans are not rich because they are better. They are rich because they invented a system of business that pushed them to conquer other people for profits. It's their system, the way they are organized, which gives them power and money.''

I was not the least bit sure Jordan understood anything of my five-hundred-year history lesson, but he nodded his head, and so I turned to the related issue. ''The second question you asked was why do they treat Africans like they do? Why do they act so superior? Is that right?''

''Yes, boss. This can be the question I am having. For my life, the European people are the bosses to us Africans and are having the money while we can be just the workers and having so little.'' He paused to collect his thoughts. ''These people can have the bad attitudes to us. They are not seeing us. They have the blindness to our lives and do not see the complications.''

''Do you think they dislike the Africans or even hate Africans?'' I probed.

''No, boss. They are not hating. They are not seeing us. We are having the life with all the difficulties of life but they cannot see us.''

''But surely, sometimes you have met. You must have interacted sometimes with Europeans. You've worked for lots of people before us. I'm sure many felt superior to you, but still you must have forced them to deal with you. I mean if you got sick or you had a need for a loan, then they would talk to you and see you were a human being with needs. Right?'' While Jordan thought for a moment, I tried to unscramble his profound remarks. ''Look, Jordan. The idea is that Europeans need to feel superior to the Africans because they are exploiting the Africans, and to exploit someone or take their money, you've got to feel superior. In other words, Europeans have to justify the system to themselves.''

I waited to see if my explanation made any sense. My ideas were certainly not new ones, but it was difficult to explain how racism, with its notions of superiority and inferiority, was one of the essential props in the system that confronted Jordan. We watched him carefully as he thought about my comments.

''These things you can speak of are very complicated, indeed, my boss. The European people can have the idea to us Africans such as to their own goodness, as you have said. But, boss, I do not see that you are understanding me.''

"What don't I understand?" I spoke quickly because I felt I had a grasp on the issue of race, and I doubted Jordan would offer any deeper insights.

"It is as you say. But it is more." He paused. "These Europeans are not seeing us, as I have said."

"I know you just said this. But I don't understand. Of course, they see you. Europeans interact with Africans, they see them, just like all of us are interacting now. We care about you a lot," I protested.

"You, my bosses, can be good people. This is true. But the European is not seeing our life," Jordan repeated himself.

"You mean the European ignores you?"

"This is the word I am now thinking is true. They ignore the African. And, my bosses, this seems to be the worst. The European cannot dislike the African. The European is just ignoring. And so the European cannot have enough attention to us to so dislike us."

I was stunned, and I sensed my friends were as well. I needed to explore his comments more fully, but I was not sure how to go about doing it. Finally, Mike spoke up. "But, Jordan, we don't ignore you. We always care about you and Ida and the kids. We talk about you and Robert and Lester all the time. So we don't ignore you. Maybe we are not as nice as we should be, but we certainly don't ignore you."

Jordan turned to Mike. "This can be true. You, my bwanas, are thinking of your Jordan and your Robert and Lester." He thought a moment, "But it can be a little bit complicated."

"How's it complicated?" John asked as quickly as I did.

Jordan thought for several minutes, and his face was flushed when he finally spoke. "This club you are going for the athletics I take to be a place for the Europeans and not the Africans. Do not these Europeans ignore us then? They are together and they do not see us. They do not care of us. They do not care of our thinking because they are doing as they wish away from the African." He thought some more. "They are not just different with the money and the ways of living but they are not seeing. I, Jordan, cannot just go with my bwanas but they cannot be thinking of my opinion. And do these rich bwanas think to the people to the village and of the difficulty of the lives? No, I do not think." Jordan was finished. His comments were piercing and powerful, and, most of all, deeply painful for us.

As someone on the receiving end of racism, he had developed far more ideas on the subject than any one of us, and we, who considered ourselves as liberal and sympathetic and certainly more decent than the British expatriate in this regard—and, in fact, worked hard at it—were confronted brutally with our own inadequacies. We too ignored the African when it was convenient, and we could not talk our way around our own shortcomings. My self-righteous quips at the expense of the European lady in the store seemed more misplaced than ever. In the final analysis, was I any different from her?

We finished the beer by the time we reached Ntcheu, but little else was spoken.

Chapter Twelve

Final Exchanges

"Robert, are you going to miss me and Mike when we leave tomorrow?"

"Yes, bwana." Robert put his coffee cup down and looked to Jordan and Lester for some support. His eyes gave a hint of a tear, and I was touched, because I sincerely believed he did not wish to see us pass from his life, presumably forever.

"Well, we're going to miss you guys, too," I said softly and looked at the three of them. Mike nodded in agreement, and the five of us remained silent for a few moments. Mike and I were excited about leaving, to be going home and to be beginning something new in our lives. This excitement had kept us from comprehending in any meaningful way what we were leaving, but this moment began to bring things into focus for me. My future was ahead of me, and I was optimistic about it and wanted to get on with it. For our three African friends, however, things would remain about the same. We would be gone from their lives, and presumably there would be a void that would be difficult to fill, at least for a while. But what about the void in our lives? Would we too find it difficult to fill, or would our new careers and new relationships simply round out our lives, neatly and easily, obliterating the past?

"Say, Robert, are you going to give me a prize for going?" Jordan and Lester immediately began to laugh, and Robert looked at them for help. "Come on, Robert, what kind of gift are you going to give us?"

"Ah no, bwana. You me give prizi. You too rich bwana. Robert poor. I no give you prizi. You give me."

"I'll give you a prizi all right. I'll give you a kick in the rear end

137

like you deserve." Jordan and Lester howled and Mike chuckled as poor Robert, knowing he was the target of my joke as usual, was forced to turn to Jordan for the translation, which Jordan was happy to supply, even going so far as to stand and kick the air for emphasis. Robert was embarrassed, but he laughed.

Mike and I had divided most of the goods we were not taking home among the three of them and Paxton, our occasional helper. What we gave away was mostly clothing, since our household goods would remain as part of the ongoing home. Jordan received the largest share of our gifts, and Mike and I had saved up enough money to give him nearly two months' wages as a bonus. People often left their servants about a 10 percent gratuity to tide the servant over until he found a new job. Jordan still had a job, so our little bonus could be used for something special. Because Mike and I were far bigger than Robert or Lester or Jordan, our clothes did not fit them, but they would have things cut down and altered, or they would trade at the market for smaller clothes. For them, it was Christmas in June, and they seemed pleased.

"I'll tell you what, Robert. Why don't you guys go catch a baby elephant and give it to us?" I smiled. Silly jokes like this always seemed to work, even though I doubted that they found them funny. It was the idea of an adult being so silly and childlike, so out of the ordinary and so peculiar, that was humorous, not the content of the joke.

Jordan shouted, "An elephant, boss? You are going to take an elephant home to Boston? This cannot be."

"Why not? What's wrong with bringing an elephant to Boston? Lots of people have elephants there."

"No, boss. This cannot be. And how can you be transporting the elephant to this place?" Jordan switched to Chichewa, and soon the three of them were laughing again.

"Look, you guys. I asked for a baby elephant, not an adult. They allow small elephants on the plane, but not big ones. They sit beside you, but of course you've got to buy them a ticket."

"Boss, you can be fooling us. The elephants are not going to the plane. No."

"Well, if you're so smart then, tell me how they got to Boston from Africa? Look, I'm telling you, they flew on a plane. How else could they get there? So, why don't you go get us one?"

Lester tried to speak, but his words were so blurred with his laughter that nothing was comprehensible. Finally, he got a few words out in Chichewa, and Jordan was able to speak for him. "My Lester here is wishing to know what the elephant is eating to the plane?"

"Leaves and groundnuts. You've got to tell them before you fly that you're bringing an elephant. Then they put the elephant's food on board. But one thing they do not allow is the elephants to drink beer because they don't want a drunken elephant. And besides the elephant would be using the toilet all the time, and this would be a problem for the people." The five of us who had shared so many of these silly stories were all laughing now.

Jordan finally spoke, "Boss, Robert here wishes to know what the elephants are doing to Boston?"

"They are used for giving people rides out to their gardens each day, or sometimes they give kids rides around for fun."

"Oh, boss, there can be automobiles for the people to go to the gardens, this I know. So these elephants cannot be for this transportation."

"Why not? They're big. You know that. They carry people all the time."

"Is it, boss? These elephants are too big?"

"Of course. Haven't you seen an elephant? They are as big as a house."

"As big as a house! No, my boss is kidding to me again."

"I'm not kidding. Ask Mike. Haven't you seen an elephant? Have Robert and Lester seen one?"

Jordan made the inquiry, and the two of them were soon shaking their heads. "No, boss, we have not seen the elephants except to the pictures. This is true."

"I believe you. It's just funny that you've never seen one since they come from around here someplace, and they are all over the place in Boston," I said.

Mike, who had been enjoying our chatter, spoke. "And what about lions? Have you seen any lions? They live around here sometimes, don't they?" Again, none of them had seen a lion. This was understandable, since the population density in this part of Malawi was so high that people would certainly confront them and eventually destroy them, but it was still strange.

"So you three Ngoni warriors have never seen a lion or an elephant, and seventy or 100 years ago your ancestors probably killed them all the time. Amazing," Mike commented. "So if you haven't seen an elephant, then I guess there's no chance of your catching one for us. If we want one, we'll just have to buy one when we get home." The session was played out.

Lester stood and went into the kitchen to make more coffee, and the four of us remained silent for a few moments. Finally, I noticed Robert looking intently out toward the dirt road that ran through the center of the boma.

"What are you looking at, Robert?" I asked.

"Ah, no," he answered.

"Ah, no what? What are you looking at?" I asked again.

Robert pointed to a woman with four small children following along behind her. He began to laugh and reached over and tapped Jordan on the arm and then pointed back at the woman.

"What's the story with the woman?" Mike asked. Robert burst into laughter again, and he rolled back in his chair. Having overheard the question, Lester came to the kitchen door, and soon he joined Robert with the laughter. Looking sheepishly at Mike and me, Jordan grinned whenever he looked at Robert and Lester.

"Come on, you guys. Explain what's so funny." Mike spoke again, "Jordan, tell us."

When the laughing subsided, he began. "Well, boss, this woman is having a child to me. It is that little one who is following there. You can see him. He is the third to the mother." Jordan pointed, and Mike stood to get a better view.

"How old's that kid?" Mike asked.

"He can be three years. This can be so."

"But, Jordan, why did you knock up this woman? Why didn't you use the magic roots?" I said.

"What is this 'knock up', my boss?"

"To make her pregnant, you know what I mean. To have a child. Why didn't you use the roots?"

"Well this can be, boss, but she is not having these roots and so she is becoming pregnant."

"Oh, that's a great story, Jordan. If someone gets pregnant, then you just say they didn't use the roots, so we can't tell if the magic works. Very clever."

"Well, this is the way. The roots can be working, but the women must be having the roots. What can I do?"

"Well, don't you feel guilty or something? I mean she's stuck with the kid, and you're free. Do you send her any money to help with the kid's support?" I asked.

"No, boss, this cannot be. This woman can be too lucky to be having a child to me. I am a handsome chap and a clever chap, too. And so this little boy is too fortunate."

"But shouldn't you help to raise the kid?" Mike spoke up.

"Why is this, boss? She is having the child and he can be a healthy one and be clever, such as me."

"You're an arrogant bastard, you know that, Jordan? And I think you're ugly and stupid, and you ought to give the woman some money," I said.

Robert and Lester burst into laughter and finally Jordan began to laugh. "Ugly and stupid. Oh, boss, you are too funny with this joke."

"Well, even if you're not ugly, you are stupid. I mean you should help to support that kid. Am I right, Lester?"

Lester stared at me from the kitchen doorway, and then he looked to Jordan for help. "The boss wants to know if I, Jordan, should be giving money to that woman to the child. What are you saying, my friend? Answer the boss."

Lester spoke in Chichewa to Jordan, but Jordan cut him off. "Answer the boss, my friend."

"No money is go to lady, boss." Lester spoke, and Jordan smiled and nodded his head.

"So, you agree with Jordan then. She should consider herself lucky to have Jordan's child. And he has no obligations to her. Man, you're as stupid as Jordan and you're ugly too."

We all laughed now. I looked at Mike, who shrugged his shoulders. We had had many similar conversations, and they all seemed to end about the same way. There was little common ground. Our attitudes about women had little in common with theirs, so our defense of the women's rights was a topic we had learned to avoid.

Jordan, I believed, did regard the woman as being fortunate to have his healthy child, and because he made no claim of fatherhood and she had complete control of the child, she had much with which to be satisfied.

"Robert, are you coming over tonight for some beer? This is the last time we can be good Africans and drink together. Everyone's coming from your house, so be sure you and Lester come too," Mike said.

"Yes, bwana," Robert replied. He waited a moment and finally addressed himself to Mike. "You give Robert trousers?"

"Shit, I already gave you three shirts. Now you want trousers. Didn't you get enough?" Mike's reply was direct. There was a hint of annoyance in his voice because he, like me, felt he had been generous, and he just did not like to be solicited, especially by friends.

It was an awkward moment, especially after two years together. Robert, who still saw us as so rich, simply could not resist asking for something more. Jordan and Lester appeared embarrassed by the quick exchange, but I could not help wondering what they really felt about it. They were more sophisticated and clever and subtle, so they would never come right out and ask for things.

Their desire for more money or material goods was understandable and I suspected that if the situation were reversed or if I had a wealthy friend, I could be happy to be the recipient of his largesse so long as I did not have to ask for it. Would I create a situation to enhance the likelihood of my receiving money or assistance? Never having been in this position, I was not sure, but I could not deny the possibility. If Jordan and Lester had manipulated us to be more generous toward them, it was under-standable given their situation.

The issue that was more troublesome was what part this inequality played in our relationship. This was an issue that had been with Jordan and me since the first day we met. How did it distort things between us? That he would want more was reason-able. That only I could decide how much to give was peculiar and was at the heart of the inequality. That I could comprehend our relationship in these terms made it all the more confusing and even raised the issue of our ability to be friends or, for that matter, of anyone's ability to have friendships, since inequalities were bound to exist nearly everywhere. And yet, from my perspective all this seemed too analytical, too sterile. We were friends. I just knew it. I could feel it. We cared for each other, and that's what mattered, and this friendship could bridge any differences of money or power or status between us. Friends were not perfect, just as friendships were not perfect. If this relationship was flawed because of some fundamental inequalities between us, then I would simply have to accept it as flawed. I would focus on the good parts of the relationship—the shared experiences, the fun, and the laughs—even though I realized that our many sad and painful days together were probably the basis of our intimacy. More importantly, I would try not to wonder about it, not to be suspicious. This must be friendship at its best. I felt it. I hoped it true.

Mike stood up and suggested that we get to the hospital for our final farewells. With this, Robert's awkward request was put behind us. Lester sat down, and I stood and went into the bedroom without comment.

"Well, achimwene, I guess it is time to board. They just announced it on the loudspeaker." My voice trembled a little as I spoke.

"Is it, boss? This can be the time for departing? Yes, I can see the people moving." Jordan's face was flushed, and his eyes appeared strained and pushed forward, and the whites around them were most obvious. His glance bounced across the waiting area as people began to gather their belongings.

I reached down and grabbed two small bags, then stood up and faced Jordan. Mike and Bill and Bernie, who had been talking at the bar with friends, quickly appeared at my side, and Jordan rose slowly, almost cautiously, to face our line of four. As the center of our attention, he appeared more awkward than I had ever seen him. Surely it was this ritual of farewells, however we would play them out, that was his immediate concern. He looked through the spaces between the four of us to the people beyond and then off to his right and then back past us.

When at last we spoke, we made short speeches full of thank-you's for the past and best wishes for the future, and we mixed our words with handshakes and giant hugs. Surprisingly, the words came easily, perhaps because they were so strongly felt or perhaps because we had rehearsed them in our minds so often that our overall ability, through words and gesture, to convey our love for our friend was obvious. It was a tender scene, but our glances, some through our tears, shot around the room as we were afraid to look directly at Jordan and to confront the heartache of a farewell that would likely be forever.

"Good-bye, my good friend, Bambo Jordan. I promise I will not forget you." I touched his face and turned quickly.

"I will not forget you, my bwana."

Chapter Thirteen

Boozing and Bossing

"Doviko."

"Yes, bwana?"

"Do you know how to make toast?" My face was expressionless as I asked, but I could see the corners of Jordan's mouth turn up.

"Toasti. Yes, I can make, bwana." Doviko appeared at the doorway of our well-lighted kitchen and looked down at Jordan and me, who were drinking beer and lounging on the little back patio.

"No, you can't, Doviko. You can't even cook water. That's what I heard." Doviko began to laugh. He was an extremely handsome and friendly man of twenty-two, fit and athletic looking, and tonight there was a hint of fear in his smile. Whenever Jordan and I were drinking, he was always at risk, and with John and Redi, our neighbors' cooks, visiting after their evening duties, he knew we had the audience we required.

"No, boss. I am cooking these days."

"Shit, Doviko. You can't cook a damn thing. I smelled the toast the other morning when Jordan was in Ntcheu. Burnt to a crisp. Completely black. *Watha* [Finished]. And you know what, Jordan? He burnt it twice before he got it right. He didn't know I saw him, but I did. It cost me a fortune just to have breakfast."

Doviko blushed at my comment, and I regretted having been so direct in front of three experienced cooks, who would understand how a young houseboy could have trouble in a modern electric kitchen.

Jordan, who had had a good deal to drink, suddenly ceased to see the humor in it all. He looked up at Doviko, his voice a bit distorted and thick. "This is disgraceful, my son. No, I cannot be teaching a stupid boy such as this to be a cook such as Jordan. For these many months this good boss is allowing me to teach you, relieving you of your duties to come to my kitchen, and you cannot make the toast. Ah, no."

I spoke quickly, "Hey, Jordan, lay off. It's only a joke, you drunk bastard. I don't give a damn about the toast. Anyone could do it."

Jordan hesitated, his face showing anger. "Is this so, boss? OK. If you are saying so. This boy can just do these things. This is the way it will be if you are saying." Jordan's tone was appalling, and John and Redi, who, I doubted, could accurately follow how our little joke turned into a snobbish put-down of Doviko, did follow things well enough to become uncomfortable.

A few moments passed, and I adjusted the shortwave radio that rested on the table where Jordan and Doviko did the ironing. I spoke softly to Jordan, "Get everyone a beer, and let's talk about something else."

Jordan yelled into the kitchen, "My son, are you hearing the boss?"

Doviko was at the door instantly. He looked down at Jordan without saying a word.

"My son, are you hearing the boss?" Jordan spoke again.

"*Iyayi* [No]."

"The boss is wanting the beer for these gentlemen and Jordan and for the boss himself. Fetch them right now, my son."

Doviko turned to do as ordered. John and Redi spoke to Jordan in Chichewa, and Jordan quickly called out to Doviko, informing him that the guests would be leaving.

I continued to play with the radio dials until Doviko appeared at the kitchen doorway with the two beers. Our guests saw this as the opportunity to make their farewells, and they quickly stood up and thanked me for the beer. Jordan and Doviko made their usual expressions of kindness to them, and they set off for their squalid sleeping quarters.

"You're rotten, you know that, Jordan? Can't you just kid with Doviko instead of acting like such a big deal and making fun of him? Try to make it funny. You treat him like some sort of slave or something. You were taught once, weren't you?"

"But, I am clever." Jordan's voice was slurred but his reply was quick.

"Yeah, you're clever all right." I paused. "What you really are is a snob and a pain in the ass, and I ought to kick you there every day to remind you."

"Is this so?" Jordan was offended but stood his ground.

"Yeah, it's so." I paused as Jordan regrouped, and I grabbed the radio to search for a clearer station. "Ah, screw it, Jordan. Let's just have some beer and listen to the radio. OK?"

"If you are saying so, boss. We can just listen." He wanted to say more, but he was forced for now to let things pass.

Soon Doviko and his new woman friend, Ada, joined Jordan and me. Doviko sat in the one remaining chair while Ada sat on the cement floor and leaned against the house and stared into the night. Ada spoke no English and had been with Doviko for only three weeks, having replaced Anni, who had stayed with Doviko for about a year. In addition to being our gardener and apprentice cook, Doviko was most importantly our night watchman, and in a country with so much poverty, one had to be concerned about robberies.

One night, Doviko had been attacked and severely slashed by four men who had attempted to rob our house, so we devised a scheme whereby Doviko guarded our house, even with its barred windows, by remaining inside. He and his lady friend slept in one end of the ranch-style house that contained the two kitchens and the dining and living rooms. My wife Claire and I, our ten-year-old son, Ian, and our four-year-old daughter, Alison, slept in the three rooms at the opposite end of the house. If we traveled, Jordan would join Doviko so that there were always two men in the house, each armed with a *panga* [machete].

A few months prior, Doviko had disqualified his short-term marriage to Anni one time when Claire and the kids and I were away. He demanded that she leave his room and leave behind all the clothes that Claire had given her. A fight of such monumental proportions took place that our neighbors, tiring of the screaming, had summoned the police. While Jordan loved to tell me the story, its sequel, with its threats of witchcraft, made Jordan uneasy and sympathetic to poor Doviko for getting himself into such a mess.

"So what did the sing'anga say yesterday when you went to pay him?" I asked Doviko as Jordan turned a curious look at me, presumably knowing the answer, but wanting Doviko to go over it aloud.

"Ah no, boss. He can just be taking the money," Doviko replied.

"You didn't speak. You just paid him then?" I asked.

"Yes, boss."

"Well, how much did he want?"

"He did not say."

"You mean he wanted to be paid, and he didn't say how much. That's strange, isn't it? How did you know what to pay?"

Jordan spoke up, "It is like this with these witch doctor men. The people can come from all this part of Malawi and they are just paying."

"Well, what are they paying? Doesn't he have prices for certain things? I mean, Doviko is being witched by Anni's family, so he goes to the sing'anga for protection. There must be a price for that service. Some range."

Doviko listened to me carefully, and then he and Jordan began to speak quickly, so that I could not follow them. Jordan spoke, "The people are saying what the value is. The people must just pay to the sing'anga what they are thinking." Doviko nodded at Jordan's explanation.

"That's wild. He cures you, and you set the price. And I suppose you pay enough so he won't be angry with you. In a way, you pay too much. Right?"

Jordan and Doviko thought for a moment. "It is just the way of this sing'anga. It is a little bit all right," Jordan rationalized.

"Well, what if you didn't pay him, or you paid too little? What then?" I pushed, but I knew their reply.

"Oh, boss, this cannot be. This is a too powerful man, and my poor Doviko, he can become so very ill from this man or from the family of the former wife who witched him. So we are paying. It is our way."

I let the conversation end. "Well, as long as it works, it makes sense. Anyway, you're square with the sing'anga, right? So you won't get sick, right?"

"Yes, bwana. I am being OK," Doviko replied softly but, it seemed, with little confidence.

A few minutes passed, and no one spoke. Doviko stared into the early evening shadows at the grass beyond the edge of the patio. Suddenly, he stood up and walked to the grass to inspect it. He pointed and spoke quickly, and Jordan and Ada rose immediately and went to his side. I joined them and soon realized that the grass was alive with ants, their columns stretching as far as I could see out into the darkness.

"What the hell is this?" I yelled.

Jordan spoke with excitement, "It is these ants, my boss. They are saying to English army ants, I am thinking."

"Army ants. They're coming right at the house. Will they eat the place down?"

"This can be, boss!"

"What can be? You mean we're not safe?" I was panicky.

While Jordan and Doviko discussed the situation, I went to get Claire and the kids so that they could witness this amazing phenomenon and prepare themselves to abandon the house should the ants choose to overrun it. They would be frightened because Alison and some of her playmates had been attacked by these big-jawed creatures while picnicking, and the five mothers were forced to remove the children's clothing amidst all the screams and to rip each ant individually from the children's skin. Claire's account conveyed their terror, but there was still admiration for the effectiveness and ferocity of these insect warriors, and observing them from a safe distance would be exciting.

As I returned to the patio with Claire and the children, Jordan, concluding a discussion with Doviko, said, "My son here is going to fetch the ashes from the quarters."

"What's that for?" Claire asked.

"It is what we are doing to the villages. These ants, they cannot be crossing the ashes. We are hoping this to be."

"So what do we do now, just get the ashes and hope?" I asked.

"Oh no, boss, this boy can just go to fetch by himself."

"Well, let's get the two buckets from in the back kitchen. We're probably going to need lots of ashes. And I'm going to help too." I turned, went inside, and returned quickly.

Doviko said nothing, but when Jordan handed him a bucket, he seemed pleased. Without hesitation, and to my astonishment, he sprinted off across the field of ants until he reached beyond what was obviously the far edge of the moving columns. Immediately, he dropped the bucket and furiously started to brush from himself what appeared to be dozens of ants, which had crawled up his legs and over his body in a fraction of a second. I could understand how a child or a slow-moving animal or any wounded creature could easily be destroyed by these insects.

"What the hell's that dumb son of a bitch doing?" I called to Jordan and then yelled across the twenty-five yards into the darkness, "Are you out of your goddamn mind?"

Doviko looked back at me, and I saw his beautiful white teeth as he grinned.

"It is these young boys, boss. They are showing that they can run so quickly that the ants cannot just catch them."

"Well, maybe. But that show-off bastard isn't going to trick me into running over those ants. It's the front door for me. Stay here, and make sure Mommy and these two are safe."

After three trips to the servants' quarters, which served the four large executive homes in our isolated neighborhood, Doviko and I had created a three- to four-inch-wide line of ashes around our house. Amazingly, the ashes did the job, and while an occasional ant would scurry across, the columns of ants generally turned back on themselves or off at oblique angles, so that the pattern of their advance was diffused and destroyed. Fascinated and relieved, we continued to watch them for an hour or more until we were sure our protective shield was working. Where the ants eventually went, I never learned. Perhaps they went back into the ground and would advance on us again.

Our evening soon quieted and went more routinely. The kids went to bed at nine, their school lessons completed and their games put away. Jordan would soon drift off to his room. His day started close to dawn, and he liked to be in bed about ten.

Jordan and I were back lounging and listening to the radio, knowing the evening would soon be over for us.

"Doviko was sort of a hero with those ashes, wasn't he?"

"Well, yes, my boss. He is doing a good job."

"Do you like Doviko, achimwene? You're nice to teach him about cooking. Most cooks wouldn't do it."

"Yes, boss, I am too fond of this boy. Well, he is a son to me."

"But you treat him badly sometimes. I try just to kid him, and he knows it. But sometimes you get a little bit mean."

"Well, this is my way. I am the father, the boss to him. So he must do as I say."

"But you do more than boss him around. You get nasty. Why?"

Jordan did not reply, so I continued, "I know why. Because you're drunk when you come home in the evening and you're embarrassed. Right?"

"What are you saying, bwana?" Jordan resented my accusation, and his voice was sharp.

"I say you two get along fine most of the time, but when you're drinking, you get mean and pick on him. That's what I say."

"No. I am simply the boss to this boy and so I am instructing him in the ways of my kitchen."

"Nonsense, Jordan. You come in here at six o'clock most nights and you're half drunk from that *kachasu* [traditional corn alcohol] junk you drink in that village at the end of the road."

"Well, this is my way. My Ida is to Ntcheu and so I am moving about after my duties. It is my habit."

"Some habit, bambo, coming in here half loaded all the time. And I'm telling you, Mommy really doesn't like it. In fact, she gets angry if you're drinking at all." I could see Jordan did not like my lecture, especially when Claire, whom he obviously liked, was his critic. I continued, "I know it's a problem to be living here without your family, and there's not much for you to do in the afternoons. But still, you can't come to work drunk."

"But I, Jordan, am doing my duties. Sure. I am not failing in my kitchen. Is the food a problem? I am asking this, my boss."

"No, the food's fine. It's just that Mommy doesn't like you half drunk when you're serving it. Hell, Jordan, why don't you just wait until after dinner, and then you can drink all the beer you want? Like tonight."

The reasonableness of my request did not take into consideration the social reality of Jordan's living as a single man far from his family or his need to socialize and to manage his free time. He said nothing.

"Why don't you go somewhere else? All you do is chase ladies and get drunk when you go to that stupid village. Why not go to town?"

"The town, boss? This is too far." Jordan thought for a moment. "The ladies can be just liking me to this place. Ida is to Ntcheu and so these ladies they are just liking me. Well, what can I do? It is so because I am handsome."

"You're a beauty, all right." Jordan seemed pleased, missing my sarcasm. I continued, "Achimwene, I don't care how many ladies you like. I just want you to drink after dinner, not before, so Mommy won't get angry."

"But I am doing my duties. The food can be fine as you are saying. I am drinking, this can be true. But I am fine and the food can be fine. So there is no problem." Jordan stopped, then looked directly at me, "So can you just be telling me, boss, what is the problem?"

"Screw you, Jordan, you arrogant little son of a bitch. I ought to fire your wise ass, you know that?"

"Well, this can be your decision." Jordan continued to look straight at me.

"You drunk bastard. I ought to whack you right in your wise-ass mouth, you mouthy bastard."

"Is this so, boss?" Jordan stood his ground.

"Get the hell out of here before I punch you one." I stood quickly and walked toward the house. Jordan set his beer bottle on the patio, then stood and stepped into the darkness without a word.

"You're too cheeky for your own good, you know that, Jordan? Mouthiest bastard in this whole goddamned country." There was no reply. I walked quickly through the kitchen. Doviko and Ada were standing at one of the counters eating their dinner, but they did not look at me as I passed, preferring to ignore the fight.

"Son of a bitch." I kept walking.

Chapter Fourteen

Prejudice Full Circle

"Kanama, come back for the kids at the regular time. Then come back again for me at about 2:15. OK?"

"This is OK, bwana." Kanama stopped the big Land Cruiser at the long flight of handsomely sculptured steps which led up to our large backyard and onto our magnificently situated home. Set on the side of the Zomba Plateau, we enjoyed a sixty-mile view across the Palombe Plain to Mount Mulanje, Malawi's truly spectacular mountain.

Like a circus show, we piled out—John McCrachen, the university's professor of history on leave from Stirling University in Scotland and his son Matthew; Ian and Alison, who had just started school; Jordan, Kanama, and I. It was market day for Jordan, and Kanama had driven to the large Zomba market to fetch him and then on to the Sir Harry Johnston Primary School to pick up the children and John, who had come from the university. His last stop was for me at the Centre for Social Research, which was located amid some of the old-style government buildings in the center of town. The tiny city of Zomba had been partially abandoned by the government when a new capital was constructed in Lilongwe. The beautiful colonial capital now contained the Chancellor College section of the university; the fisheries and forestry research departments; the statistics and census departments; a large general hospital; the country's only hospital for the mentally ill; the parliament buildings, which were used only a few weeks a year; the government printing office; a large social club; a small government hotel; and the offices of the Malawi Certification and Testing Board, which conducted the examinations for school promotions.

Kanama went to the back of the vehicle, opened the double doors, and began pulling out the large baskets that Jordan had spent the morning filling with fruits, vegetables, meats, and fish.

"Yao, *bwelani kuno* [come here]," he yelled when he spotted Doviko at the top of the stairs. Doviko sprinted down to Kanama, and I could see that the playful Kanama was about to have some fun.

Doviko clapped his hands together gently and greeted Kanama with great politeness.

"You are not saluting me, Yao. I am the general. Are you not learning to salute the general as you were to the Young Pioneers?"

Doviko quickly came to attention, and gave Kanama a full military salute. Kanama pulled on Doviko's shirt and walked around him, conducting an inspection, and began to speak rapidly in Chichewa. Jordan smiled at the two of them, and Doviko at last grabbed two of the baskets and hauled them up the stairs to the house. I took the third basket, and Jordan and Kanama followed, empty-handed. Kanama stood on the patio outside the kitchen door as Jordan and Doviko and I began to unpack the baskets.

"Why do you guys always pick on poor Doviko?" I directed myself to Kanama.

"Ah, it is these Yao people, bwana," Kanama spoke up. He and Jordan began to laugh until Kanama mumbled something which sent them into a howl.

"What's so funny?" I asked again.

"It is these Yao people, boss. Ah, I cannot say," Kanama responded poorly but regained some of his composure.

"What do you mean, it is these Yao people? What's wrong with Yao people, you prejudiced bastards?"

"Well, they are as they are," Jordan spoke.

"What's that mean?" I asked.

Jordan continued, "Well, they are different to us Ngoni people such as Mr. Kanama here and to myself. Well, they are like that. This we can see. It is a little bit like that."

"A little bit like what? Because some Yaos are Muslims. Or because they were slave traders while you great Ngoni people were warriors kicking the hell out of everybody for fifty years. Is that the difference?"

"Yes, we are the greatest warriors in all Malawi. The best to all of Africa." Kanama spoke up playfully, but with obvious pride. He continued, "The Yao people cannot just capture we Ngoni. We are the most fierce warriors and we will destroy you, is this not so, Mr. Dama?"

"Mr. Kanama is speaking the truth, boss. The Ngoni are the best warriors to Malawi for all the time. These Yao people they cannot be capturing we Ngoni. No."

"That's a hundred years ago. What about now? You don't seem to be so different now. Are you richer than the Yaos? Are you more powerful than they are?" I let Kanama and Jordan think for a moment. "Aren't the Ngoni people and the Yaos just both farmers today, peasants? To me, no one seems better."

Kanama spoke quickly in Chichewa, and he and Jordan again broke into laughter while Doviko, face flushed, simply continued to unpack the baskets. Finally Kanama said, "These Yao people are not like us. Yaos like Ngoni people? No." He and Jordan burst into laughter again a third time. "They are *gule wamkulu* these people," Kanama blurted out.

"What do you mean, gule wamkulu? You mean those dancers who wear the masks are Yaos?"

"Yes, bwana. The dancers are gule wamkulu," Kanama replied.

"So what? They are just traditional dancers, aren't they?"

"Gule wamkulu," Kanama became excited. "Yao, explain to the bwana here of this gule wamkulu."

Doviko's face showed embarrassment. He turned to me for relief.

"Why don't you explain, Kanama, since you know so much?" I came to Doviko's aid.

Again, Kanama and Jordan went into a conversation that excluded me but embarrassed poor Doviko. Judging that Doviko would not speak, Kanama finally made a half-hearted reply. "These are the very dangerous witch people. Very dangerous, my bwana. No, you must be watching, or they can catch you, just like that. Finished." He snapped his fingers. "Is this not so, my good Phiri?" He spoke to Jordan for support.

"This is so, boss. These gule wamkulu people can be too very dangerous," Jordan answered.

"So what do they do exactly?"

"This we cannot be knowing. It is their secret. Is this not so, my Yao friend?" Kanama was still after Doviko.

"You mean they're a secret society?" I asked.

"Oh, they are too secret. We Ngoni cannot be knowing such things. But this boy here he is knowing. He is a Yao, so he can know," Kanama continued.

"I am not knowing," Doviko spoke finally, and he spoke seriously. "It is just for some of the people. I, Doviko, am not knowing of these things."

Kanama spoke so quickly to him in Chichewa that I could not follow, but I spoke up. "Knock it off, will you, you guys? Leave the poor bastard alone." I continued, "You two fierce Ngoni warriors are the two most prejudiced characters I've met in a long time. You should know better. It's the same stuff said about African people by whites, and you should stop it."

"What is this, boss?" Jordan asked.

"Prejudice. You say you and Kanama are better than Doviko because he is Yao. That's stupid, and you don't like it when white people say things like that about you. Right?"

"This is true, boss," Jordan said.

"So why say it?"

Kanama and Jordan spoke to each other and did not appear the least bit shamed by my scolding. They laughed again, and Kanama spoke: "But these Yaos are not as we Ngoni. No."

"You guys are hopeless bigots. Only your people are good, and everyone else is bad. That right?"

"Well, what can we say, boss? The Ngoni people are the best warriors to Malawi. And, so it is like that." Jordan's words appeared final.

It was my turn to speak. "Even though I lived in Ntcheu for two years, I hereby declare myself a Yao, and I'm going to come around and bewitch the living shit out of you two if you don't stop being so mean to poor Doviko."

"My boss, a Yao!" Jordan blurted out amidst the laughter.

"And Mommy and Ian and Alison are going to be honorary Yaos so they can help me fix you two."

"Ian and Alison are Yaos," Jordan bent over in laughter while Kanama dashed toward the stairway so as not to laugh directly in front of me.

I yelled after him, "Get the hell out of here. Keep going, Ngoni warrior. You bigot."

In moments, Kanama had backed the vehicle from the garage and was headed down the long drive. I could see a big smile on his face. He had enjoyed the exchange.

"Now we've got you, Jordan, and we are going to fix you because you are so rotten."

"Boss?" Jordan replied. He returned to unpacking the supplies.

"Don't boss me, Jordan. I always knew you were a no-good snob, but now I see you're a bigot besides. Screw you and Kanama. We are Yaos here from now on."

Jordan did not react to my comments but merely continued to put the supplies away.

"Say, Jordan. After we leave Malawi and you're looking for a job, would you work for a rich bwana if he was a Yao?" I asked, sincerely.

"Jordan work for a Yao? No, boss."

"Why not? I mean, if you needed a job. And you didn't have any money."

"No, I cannot do this job."

"What if you were hungry, starving? Then you'd have to work for anyone who would employ you. Right?"

"I cannot be doing the cooking to these people. No."

"What if you had no choice? You were hungry. Then what?" I repeated.

"No, I cannot."

"God, Jordan. I suppose you wouldn't work for any other African either? Even the president of Malawi!"

"I am just the cook to the Europeans, my boss. These small boys, they can be the cooks for the African people. But as for me, I am the cook to the Europeans."

"Well. What if you were hungry? Then would you cook for a Malawi bwana? You would then, wouldn't you?"

"I am the cook to the European people only. This I know."

"Damn it, Jordan. I'm asking if you were starving and needed to work. Then would you do it?"

"No, I cannot. It is not for a cook such as Jordan to cook to these African people."

Exasperated, I walked away. "You're a racist, Jordan. And you're trapped in your own prejudice."

Chapter Fifteen

No Chances

"Jordan, this is Ben Kaluwa. Ben, this is my friend Jordan."

"Hello, sir," Jordan spoke very politely and bowed his head ever so slightly.

"Hello, Jordan," Ben reached out his hand and Jordan shook it hesitantly.

"Bwana Ben is an economist at the university, Jordan. And we worked on a few projects together."

"I see. This is very interesting, my boss." Jordan spoke in his most serious tone and with a most thoughtful face, but he could add no more. An awkward moment was averted when Ben turned to Jordan and, in Chichewa, asked him where his village was. Immediately Jordan brightened and the two began conversing, and I turned to John Banda, the barman, and ordered three beers.

The small bar at the government-run hostel was crowded this night with men from the Zomba community. Most were high-status civil servants, and several were faculty members from Chancellor College. (The college included the liberal arts faculty as well as the schools of law, public administration, and education.) Normally the bar attracted a small crowd, since both travelers and locals enjoyed the open khonde which connected the bar to both a comfortable sitting room and a large dining room in the main building. The setting was attractive, and the customers could look down upon well-manicured lawns, flower gardens, and a variety of tropical and semi-tropical trees.

Jordan and Ben seemed to be enjoying each other's conversation. As I sat on the one remaining bar stool, I could hear them switch to another language and continue to talk. I passed them their beer, paid Banda, and still they continued.

"Hey, what language are you guys speaking?"

"Shona," Ben answered and smiled. Like many Malawians, Ben had grown up in Zimbabwe, formerly Rhodesia, and was fluent in the major language of that region. "This guy is amazing. He speaks Shona as well as I do, and he hasn't been there in thirty years." Ben's compliment was not lost on Jordan. Ben continued. "Hell, he speaks Ndebele too and a whole lot of Malawian languages. He even speaks Ngoni, and not many people can do that anymore."

Ben immediately spoke in another language, presumably Ndebele, and Jordan responded with ease. Ben was impressed. While many Africans spoke three languages, in some fashion or other, few had Jordan's superior level of fluency in so many languages.

While Ben was a truly likeable colleague, I was amazed to see that he was sincerely interacting with a man of dramatically lower status than himself. It was something few elite Malawians would do. Ben had a cook himself, and I wondered if he had ever interacted with him as he was now with Jordan. Most cooks I knew would resist coming to a place with men of Ben's stature, but Jordan accepted my invitation without hesitation, but with the assurance that I would slip him a few kwachas so that he could do some buying.

Soon Ben and Jordan were seated at a small table with three other men, and I began a conversation with two friends from the university. Occasionally, I glanced toward Jordan to see that he appeared to be doing well, listening carefully, and speaking if addressed.

Simon, the waiter, was a man blessed with the proper personality for the position in this place where powerful men often drank and talked too much, a place where secrets were meant to be kept, or at least judiciously passed along. Simon was rumored to be a spy for either party officials or the special branch of the police; and his assignment, I suspected, was to report on political complainers. If true, his job as a conduit for information was done superbly, as there was little margin for error, and failure would quickly lead to his removal. His job as a waiter he did well too, and by Malawian standards he obviously made a good wage, augmented by generous tips from foreign travelers.

This evening, Simon was busy carrying drinks out to the guests on the khonde or in the sitting room. He stopped at the end of the bar as John set about filling his order. He attempted to speak to me, but there were two Europeans, whom I had never seen before, between us. He stepped behind them to speak to me.

"Who is this gentleman with you, bwana?"

"He's my friend, Jordan Dama. Why?"

"I am just asking," Simon continued.

"But why are you asking?" I answered and smiled.

"I am just knowing these things."

"You're a nosy bugger, you know that, Simon?" He did not like my remark, but I continued. "Hey, he's just a good friend of mine."

"I am hearing he is the cook boy to you," Simon said.

"Yes, he's my cook, but he's also my friend. For almost twenty years now."

Simon, of course, knew the answer to his question before he asked it. I suspected that he disapproved of Jordan's being here and mixing with such an exalted crowd, so I tried to give him little satisfaction. Shortly, he stepped back and stood at the end of the bar.

Jordan appeared behind me and ordered beer for himself and the men at his table. I could see the quick glances of some in the room as he reached into his pocket for the money. He handled the exchange well, although the laborious count of his change as he picked the coins from the bar hinted at his apprenticeship as a big spender. He carried four beers to the table and returned for his own beer. To my amazement, he began to speak in German to the two men to my left. They turned to speak, and their smiles indicated that they were pleased to find someone who could speak their language. The conversation was brief, but everyone in the bar was aware of it, and I sensed they were as amazed as I. As Jordan turned and joined the men, all eyes seemed to follow him.

The two Germans, I soon learned, were pilots who had delivered a new plane from Germany. They would be returning home on a commercial flight the next night.

The evening for Jordan and me lasted about an hour more. Ben approached me twice. First, he conveyed his admiration for Jordan's ability to mix socially with men like himself. Second, he told me that Jordan's language abilities were most remarkable, unlike those of anyone else he had ever met. These were genuine compliments, and I suspected Ben and the others had, in some way, informed Jordan. As we made our farewells, Jordan seemed pleased with himself, even a bit elated.

Getting into my car, I asked, "Did you have fun tonight?"

"Oh, it is a wonderful night, my boss. I take these men to be very good gentlemen."

"So you like big bwanas, do you? And what makes you think they're nice guys? Maybe they beat their wives or drink too much."

"Well, I cannot say. But I take them to be clever gentlemen."

"What's clever? You're as smart as they are. Don't you think so?"

"Oh no, boss. These men can be too educated. Not such as me."

"Well, they may be educated, but that doesn't mean they're so smart. You can be smart and not have gone to school. Some of your ancestors were smart, and they didn't go to the university.''

Jordan thought for a moment. "Well, this is so. Those are clever people who have very little schooling.''

"Like you. You're smart and only went to old standard three. Hell, you can speak more languages than all those guys put together. And, I am sure, you are as intelligent as anyone there.''

"Yes, this is true, boss.''

"Well, it was sure hard to convince you of that,'' I joked, but Jordan remained serious. I turned the car up our long driveway toward the garage. "The real question is why you are a cook and they are big bwanas. Especially since you're as smart as they are.''

We got out of the car, and I closed the garage doors. Doviko appeared at the top of the steps and greeted us, but we made it clear we were going to talk; so he returned to the house.

I continued, "Do you see the question I'm asking? Why are some people bwanas and some poor peasants, or cooks like you?'' I waited. "From what we can see tonight, it's probably not intelligence, since you're smart too. Right?''

"This can be, boss.''

"So, how do you explain it?''

Jordan thought for a moment, and I sat on the stone railing of the steps. "It is like this,'' he finally spoke.

"What does that mean? Not the old argument that God wants it that way. That God made some rich and some poor.''

"It is confusing, boss. This I can know.''

"Come on, my smartso friend. How do you explain why a few people are bwanas, and most are just poor folks?'' I pointed my finger and continued, "And don't say 'that is the way,' or I'll smack you for being so stupid.''

Jordan smiled and became serious again. He leaned back against the stone rail opposite me. He began to speak several times but stopped. It was a very difficult question, and he seemed unequipped to conceptualize a good explanation. Finally, he said, "Say, boss, I was just perhaps thinking that I could be enjoying a beer with the boss before retiring.''

I laughed aloud. "You're a smart one, Jordan. As soon as you can't answer, you change the topic and turn to alcohol.'' I laughed again and soon we were sitting on our little back khonde joined now by Doviko and Ada and our two beers.

"So how do you explain it, Jordan? If it's not intelligence that makes you a bwana, is it luck?''

Puzzled, Doviko asked Jordan about our conversation, and Jordan went into a long and animated explanation that I could not follow. Doviko, after listening carefully, seemed to have no reaction.

I wondered if he too viewed social inequality as natural or whether it was too painful to comprehend, or whether it was such a new topic that he had no opinions.

"Come on, Jordan. Is it luck? Some are lucky and most are not?" He thought for several minutes, long minutes. The idea of luck and coincidence, I guessed, was not very appealing to him because its nature was so statistical and mathematical. So, when he failed to reply, I again pushed him. "What's wrong with luck to explain it?"

But again he hesitated. Then he turned to Doviko and spoke rapidly. Doviko shook his head gently but would not look at me. Jordan, apparently supported, spoke. "No, the luck cannot be the reason."

"Then, my good achimwene, are you saying it is God's idea to make some very rich and some horribly poor like most of these poor village people?"

"No, boss, I am just saying it is the way. This I can just see."

The conversation was stuck. Jordan, like most people, could not explain his life very well. Rather, he saw things as natural and normal.

Finally he asked, "What is the boss saying?"

Both he and Doviko looked at me, and I smiled and then laughed gently. "It's power and then money. The chiefs had power, so there were big people and little people. Then there were the colonials, who stole much of the people's land and had guns to back them up. Then there are the new Malawian bwanas, some who are now rich and who use the laws that they have made themselves to help them be rich." I looked to see if they were interested and then continued. "It has to do with the system, the economic system, the money. The question is: who are the people who control the money of Malawi? Who has the big estates? How did they get the money? Why do they keep all the money and the workers have so little?"

I could see Jordan and Doviko listening carefully. My discussion was not exactly new to them. They knew Europeans were privileged and that there were now some rich and influential Malawians and a few others in a type of middle class. I continued, "So you can see it's the system and not just a natural thing. God didn't just make some rich and some poor. People made it that way."

They both stared at me. My explanation was too brief and too abstract, and I sensed there was little point in trying to go on.

They sat in silence like school kids who did not know what to say, and Jordan sipped his beer. They exchanged a few words quietly, and I waited, curious to see if comments would follow to my little lecture on political economy.

Finally, Jordan said, "Well, what you have told us is very interesting, my boss. My son here and I am thinking this to be so."

"But you don't really understand it, right?"

"Yes, boss. We are not just understanding," Jordan spoke and Doviko nodded in agreement.

"Don't feel bad. Most people wouldn't understand, and the ones that did probably wouldn't agree." I laughed and they smiled. While the quiz was nearly over, I decided to make a last comment. "Those bwanas at the hostel are all very educated men, right?"

"Yes, boss. I have explained this to my son here."

"Some of them went to the university in the United States or England, and some to the university here in Malawi. Now the thing that makes them big bwanas is that they are educated and they can get good jobs. Right?"

"Yes, boss," Jordan spoke and Doviko nodded.

"I'll bet not one of those men comes from the village, like you two. None are sons of peasants. Understand?"

Their glances to me seemed empty, so I continued. "Look, I know of no bwanas whose fathers or uncles were not little bwanas already, like postal employees or men in the public works. It is too difficult for the child of a poor farmer to succeed in school. The kids drop in and out of school because the school fees are too high for most parents. And the schools in the rural areas are often very poor, with mostly unqualified teachers. Right?"

They shook their heads in agreement.

"Even you, Jordan, haven't sent all your kids through school, and you have a little money. So, most parents cannot do it, right?"

Again, they assented.

"You've got to go to the best schools, whether at a mission school or a government school. Your parents must have the fees. The father must have a job, and the family usually does not live in the village. Even Doviko, whose village is close by, went only to Standard 8, and he went to a good primary school. The kids from the rural areas have no chance." I waited a moment. "Look, I am sure some village kids have become bwanas, but not many."

"I am thinking this is true," Jordan reflected quietly and looked to Doviko for support.

"So you can see that the bwanas have a better chance to make their children bwanas too. They have money, and so their kids get the best chance. The rural farmer's kid has little chance." I waited again. "So the people with money, the bwanas, do the best. As I said, it is the economic system, the money, that directs how you succeed. Maybe it's a little luck or hard work too, but for sure it isn't natural or God's law that some are rich and most poor." My lecture was over. My example, I thought, was reasonable; and as intelligent men, conversant with the educational system, I was confident they would understand. And so I lectured them no more, and they seemed relieved when I stopped.

Jordan and I had another beer, but we said little. Doviko played with the radio until Jordan stood and announced that he was retiring.

"Thank you for a wonderful evening, my boss."

"Sure thing, Bambo Jordan. It was fun. And you really put on a show for the guys at the hostel."

"Is this so, boss?" Jordan's face was radiant.

"Yes, this is so," I said matter-of-factly.

"Ndapita."

"OK. Gonani bwino. And try to figure out why they're rich and you're not." I smiled, and Jordan did too.

"Well, the things are just as they are," he answered softly and turned.

"Maybe you're right, good friend. Good night."

"Good night, boss."

Chapter Sixteen

For The Children

"There he is, Kanama. And we're almost on time."

Kanama slowed and carefully turned the Land Cruiser gently to the right off the tarmac and onto the dirt roadway that ran along the front of Ntcheu's row of shops. The place had changed little in eighteen years, but the Indian traders were now gone, forced by the government to own shops only in the cities. It was difficult to judge whether Ntcheu had suffered because of this policy. Several of the twenty or so shops were closed along the strip, but to the south near the boma new shops had opened. The shops themselves remained the same. Fronted by large covered khondes where the tailors still worked, these cubes of concrete were edifices of the most practical and crudest architecture imaginable. Some twenty feet high, they resembled fortresses with windows covered by strong steel bars. As places of commerce they stood to protect their cherished goods and to remind the Africans that cash transactions to obtain the merchants' treasures would be difficult. I had heard all the whispered remarks from exiled Indian merchants in Zomba about the Malawians' inability to merchandise, but it seemed that while some Malawians had failed, others had done fine. The peasants, for their part, were simply confronted by black-faced entrepreneurs instead of brown-faced ones, and I guessed things were much as they had always been. Kanama stopped the cruiser and Jordan, who was sitting on the steps of the shop, stood up and waved to us.

I got out with Kanama and Benson Kandoole, an economist trained in the United States, who was returning with me from a three-day meeting in Lilongwe. We all greeted Jordan.

"Not too bad, Jordan. Six o'clock and I guessed half-five. If it

167

hadn't been for Bwana Benson here, who insisted upon buying beer for all his friends up in Dedza, we would have been on time. And, of course, Kanama had to give a lift to half the people in Dedza, since he's a big mfumu up there. Jordan and Benson smiled. Jordan then turned and grabbed his small suitcase and his basket of flour.

As Kanama went to the back of the vehicle to open the doors, he announced, "I am the chief to all the Ngoni people. And so I am just helping them." His voice was playful, as it often was.

"He drives ninety miles an hour and stops ten times when we come through Dedza to say hello to all his kinsmen, so we average twenty miles an hour. Great driver, this great *Nkosi* [Chief]." I spoke so Kanama would not have the last word.

Jordan's case and basket were placed in the vehicle alongside our luggage and two large baskets of potatoes that we had bought along the roadside. Kanama locked the doors while we all climbed into the cruiser.

"A couple of more roadies, Benson, to get us to Balaka?" I asked.

"Good idea," Benson smiled. He and I had been drinking beer since we left Lilongwe, having developed a scheme on previous trips whereby we would stop in one of the old town bars as we left the city and would buy two beers each. Then we would stop every fifty miles or so as we traveled south, stopping at roadside huts serving as bars with kerosene refrigerators. Kanama never drank alcohol, whether on duty or off, so we were fortunate in that regard.

"To the Ever Rest, bwana Kanama. We have to get Phiri a beer. Right, Jordan?" Jordan agreed readily, and Kanama raced along to a large bar, set some thirty yards back from the road, which accommodated the thirsty passengers in the large lorries and the many cars that, surprisingly, could be found there at most any time. The Ever Rest Restaurant and Bar had not been in operation when I lived there eighteen years before, but I had visited it when I stayed several days in Ntcheu while conducting a project evaluation for the Ministry of Community Development. Bar, restaurant, truck stop, and whorehouse all in one, and its multipurpose set of activities combined in one place probably made sense, given the resources.

Kanama pulled directly to the front door of the large bar, which had been painted lime green and trimmed in red and yellow, like a flag of some new nation. The four of us stepped out, and I took our four empty beer bottles to make the exchange. The three of them followed me into the large bar.

It was just dusk outside, and the two overhead electric lights in the bar were very inadequate for the large interior. The loud sounds of kwela music blared from a giant radio prominently placed along an interior wall. As I struggled to see better in the room, I became aware of a group of some twenty individuals who stopped to stare at us. I marched to the bar and passed the four bottles over to the barman as Kanama and Jordan and Benson joined me.

"I'll have three Greens and a Fanta for now. And when we leave, I want six Greens to go. So figure in these returns, OK?" The barman hesitated, and Benson quickly spoke up in a mixture of Chichewa and English to explain my request.

The drinks were quickly placed on the bar, and I passed over the notes to cover the cost. The four of us turned to survey the crowd, a segment of modern Africa not mentioned in the tourist brochures—neither the modern elite with their bright smiles, fancy clothes, and new cars nor the poor villagers, silently struggling for so little, or nothing. Instead, these were the petty wage earners, the proletariat, of Malawi. Rural schoolteachers, postal clerks, health assistants, small shopkeepers, artisans, mechanics, clerks, policemen, drivers, and messengers. Then, too, there were the peddlers and hustlers, the pimps and prostitutes, the dealers and schemers, the robbers and con men, all separated from village life but incapable of making it in Malawi's small wage economy without cunning and a selfish individualism that further separated them from traditional life.

It was a common scene: a few drunks with many more soon to be that way, a few souls showing off by being present, a few hustling for drinks, a few hustling for sex, as buyers or sellers. Although they dressed inexpensively, these people had flair, which made a statement about their relatively high status in the community. The women wore tight-fitting dresses embossed with bright flower prints or pictures of Dr. H. Kamuzu Banda, the life president. To complete the look, they wore plastic shoes of yellow or red or green. The older men were in trousers and the teenagers in shorts, without shoes. All wore long-sleeved shirts, which seemed their badge of status. It was the underside of developing Africa, or even all the Third World, and while the developed world had its equivalents, the scene was more pitiful here.

I watched two attractive bar girls dancing slowly with two likely customers. One, whose dress was so short and tight that I began to stare at her, looked at me and smiled, and I gave her an exaggerated grin and a big wave in return. Several other bar girls and young men who had clustered near us at the bar laughed aloud at my antics, the coquettish dancer having been exposed by my playful response. Benson and I smiled at each other, and two of the girls stared at me with most flirtatious and sexy looks. Benson began to chuckle. "Is it me or my money?" I asked.

"Definitely your money." Benson was about to laugh when a girl came up to my side and quickly rubbed my arm as she rubbed her body against my side and leg. It was quite a scene, and I was embarrassed and stepped back.

Benson spoke again. "An old friend of yours, it seems to me." Jordan and Kanama held back their smiles to see how I would react.

"Say, lady. Muli bwanji?" A ridiculous question, but all the bar girls and their friends seemed to be enjoying the show as much as my friends.

"Tili bwino, bwana," she answered gently and moved toward me and grabbed my arm again.

"I'm a happily married man, lady. Don't take advantage of me just because I'm on business." Benson laughed, but the others continued to stare with great interest. "Do you speak English?" I asked while she began to rub herself against me again. "*Dzina lanu ndani?*" I tried again.

"Losi," she replied.

"Losi, that's a nice name," I muttered as all eyes were now focused on me. "Say, Losi, would you like a beer? *Kodi, mufuna mowa?*"

I turned quickly to the barman, who had been watching with considerable amusement. Without my asking, he handed Losi a beer and a small plastic glass.

Kanama, Jordan, Benson, and the group of onlookers were thoroughly enjoying both Losi and me, so I let her take a few sips before reaching out and shaking her hand.

"Bye, bye, Losi. Ndapita." I smiled and reached out and patted her arm. She smiled, and I turned away quickly. "Let's go sit out on the back veranda and finish these." I walked across the dark dance area, and my friends followed me to an open khonde containing four wooden tables and some sturdy chairs. The area was well lighted, and our view was eastward, toward dozens of villages where I had worked years before. Even Jordan's village was out there someplace.

From the khonde a long hallway led along the rear of the building to a series of rooms for the travelers and the girls. We sat silently for a while. Occasionally a girl would peek from the doorway to the bar and giggle and then retreat quickly to continue her laughing. I figured few bwanas and fewer white ones came here; therefore, I was the source of their amusement. So if I got the chance, I would make a face, and their giggles would change to laughter and entice some new girls to come have the crazy azungu make a face at them.

"The ladies can be very amused, my boss," Jordan said.

"They're crazy about you, Bruce," Benson added. I chuckled, and he went on, "You could really make one of them happy." Then he laughed along with Kanama and Jordan.

"Not me, I'm afraid," I said. "I've got no problems with them.

Just some sympathy. It must be rough in bars like this. I'm sure they get paid hardly anything. Sad scene."

Benson readily agreed. Kanama and Jordan simply stared at me. I assumed they had never given prostitution much thought, perhaps thinking that bar girls, too, were a natural part of the social fabric.

We finished our drinks and decided to move along. The barman placed the six cold bottles on the counter as we passed and, as I went to get them, my flirtatious friend again gave me a smile. Quickly, I gave her a big hug, and the crowd of onlookers laughed openly. Benson tried to smile politely as I handed him his beers; playing with the pretty bar girl was something he would never do, and his smile seemed to mask his disapproval.

In minutes we were speeding southward in the dark at eighty miles an hour. This main road was constructed so that drivers could see great distances ahead, and I regarded Kanama as a very safe and always sober driver. The last eighty miles would go by quickly if we did not stop for more beer in Balaka or Liwonde.

Three days earlier, we had dropped Jordan off on our way north so that he could visit his family and hire help to do some heavy cultivating. The rainy season would soon be starting, and the fields must be ready. Ida was incapable of doing all the heavy work alone. I was ready to hear how his visit had been.

"How were Ida and the kids, Jordan?" I asked.

"Very good, sir."

"Did you get your business done?"

"Oh, yes, my boss. I have employed two young chaps for the cultivation."

"Are these kids from your village?"

"Well yes. They are the nephews to my Ida. As you know, it is to the village of Ida that I am having my house."

"How old are these kids?" I asked.

"I should say they can be thirteen, boss. Yes. They can be so."

"If you don't mind, achimwene, how much do you pay them?"

"Oh, they are just young boys, my boss."

"Come on, you cheap bastard, how much do you pay them?" I turned and looked back at Jordan. Benson, sitting beside him, smiled.

"No, boss, they are just boys. So they can be just assisting."

"You don't pay them. There must be days and days of hard work. Come on. Do you give them ten kwacha or twenty, or what?" I could see Kanama in the darkness. Like Benson, he too was smiling.

"No, no, boss. This can be too much. For these young boys. Ten kwacha. No."

"Well how much then? Come on."

"They are just the nephews to my Ida. So they are just doing."

"How much, Jordan? You've got to give them something."

"Well, it is just a few kwacha, my boss."

"What's a few?"

"Well it can be one."

"One. You rotten no good son of a bitch, Jordan. You've got to be the cheapest bwana in all of Malawi." Benson and Kanama laughed aloud, but as I turned forward, I could see that Jordan was not laughing. I continued, "Cheap, cheap, bwana."

Jordan protested. "These are just small boys."

"What do you think, Kanama?" I turned and asked.

Kanama hesitated, glanced at me and spoke, "Mr. Dama here is fair."

"Sure, you guys have jobs, but you won't give any away to the poor people. Right?"

"Bwana, the payment to the boys is fair. Sure," Kanama spoke again.

"What do you think, Benson? You're the economist," I sought help.

"I think it's OK. They are boys, and they are of his family. So anything is OK. I'm sure he'll share some of the food if they need it. He is not really paying them as employment per se. It's a gift, a present, to one another."

I turned around and looked at the two of them. "Well, I expected these two cheap Ngoni warriors to stick together, Benson. But now you've left me the odd man out. So I concede. I apologize, Jordan. I now realize that you're a very generous man." Benson and Kanama smiled, but Jordan remained as serious as ever. I continued, "So how much would a generous man like you pay for a girl at the Ever Rest?"

"Me, boss?" Jordan looked surprised. "I am not giving money to the women such as these."

"You used to be a temporary driver along here when they were putting in the road. So you know all the places. Right?" I pushed him.

"This can be. But I do not pay these women." He hesitated. "This can be impossible for me. Paying the women. No. They can be paying Jordan."

Benson and Kanama laughed instantly, and Kanama said something in Chichewa that made them laugh even more. Jordan remained serious.

I said, "God's gift to women, this one."

"Well, it is true, boss. The women are too fond of your Jordan. True."

"So how many girlfriends do you have in Zomba?" I asked.

"Oh, boss, it is not like that. I can have my Ida for these many years."

"Ida and a few girlfriends, perhaps," I laughed as I replied. Kanama and Benson, I sensed, were enjoying the conversation.

"Well the ladies can be enjoying me. This I can say," Jordan spoke confidently.

"And how many kids did all this enjoyment add up to?"

"What is this, boss?"

"How many children with all this enjoyment?" I repeated my question.

"How many children am I having? Is this the question?"

"That's it."

"Oh, I should say twenty."

Kanama howled in laughter, and Benson smiled and shook his head ever so slightly.

"Twenty? Are you crazy? They should lock you up," I said.

"Well. This is the way. I am having three to my previous wife. You have met the oldest. The one called Wili, who has come to visit to Zomba. And I am having ten children to my Ida. The others, well, they are just here and there with the women who are enjoying your Jordan."

"Are you counting the women next door that you knocked up?"

"Who is this, boss?"

"What's her name? Mazumda's housegirl."

"Oh, I am forgetting this one. But she is just a bit pregnant to this time. So it can be twenty."

I did not know if it was fair to push the conversation any further. Jordan and I were close friends, but Benson and Kanama were basically strangers, and Jordan's personal life was for him to disclose, not for me. I said nothing more. Twenty minutes later, Benson asked, "Are you supporting these children, Mr. Dama?"

Jordan stared straight ahead. "No, bwana, I am not supporting. These children can be just with the mothers."

Benson said no more. We drove on for some time before I finally spoke. "I'll bet I know your argument about not helping these kids out, Jordan. These women are lucky to be having your children since you're such a handsome and clever fellow. Right?"

"This can be true, boss." Jordan answered seriously. I could see giant smiles on Benson's and Kanama's faces.

We drove on in silence until Benson again spoke up. "Did you ever hear of zero population growth and family planning, Mr. Dama?"

"What is this, bwana?"

"Limiting the number of your children. Controlling your family size so that each couple has two children or one for each parent. This way the population won't grow."

"To have few children? Is this it?" Jordan turned to Benson.

"Yes. Right. Have you ever thought of that?"

"No, bwana. This I cannot just imagine. Are you knowing of this, Mr. Kanama?" Jordan tried to engage an ally.

Kanama, the bachelor, shook his head and he uncharacteristically kept still. I wondered if the topic was too sensitive for him.

"The idea is for families to have fewer children so that the land will not be overrun with people. If there are too many people, then there won't be enough land and food for everyone. See?" I added to Benson's explanation.

"I am not understanding, my boss. We must be having many babies. It is our way," Jordan remarked sincerely.

"So they can take care of you when you are an old man and so you can prove what a stud you are, right?" I said.

"What is 'stud', my bwana?"

"A powerful maker of babies. Someone who is good at making women pregnant. That's sort of a stud."

"Well, if I am understanding, the reasons you are stating are true." Jordan hesitated a moment. "But, boss, the babies are just dying so many times. So many children are good for us. And the big people are passing away too fast. This population of which bwana Kandoole is speaking I am not understanding."

I spoke up. "Jordan, the number of people in Malawi is clearly growing too fast. In the eighteen years since I was first here, the number of people has almost doubled. Benson here is an economist, and he knows all these numbers about the population getting bigger. And the problem is that the number of schools and hospitals and teachers and doctors hasn't doubled. So people are worse off. Understand?"

"But I am confused, my boss. All the friends to Ntcheu are gone. Robert, Lester, Paxton. I am the only one now. So the babies are taking the places to the earth. Is this not so?"

"Well, yes. But the number of babies grows faster than the number of adults who die at any time. So the population just gets bigger and bigger. And everyone's worse off."

"I am not understanding. The babies can be a goodness to us," he protested.

"Mr. Dama," Benson spoke up politely. "Why are there these bar girls? Why are so many men from Malawi working in the mines in South Africa? Why are the villages empty of most men like you?"

Jordan thought for a moment. "It can be the way of the life here. I am thinking."

Benson went on. "Well, it's complicated, but one thing is that there are too many of us Malawians, and we can't all survive on the land, at least not with our current productivity."

"But the babies who are living can be the children who can work to the gardens," Jordan added.

"Good point. It's true that older children and healthy adults can produce more than they eat. But we have land shortages with too many people; and even if you could work, there's not enough space, so productivity remains low. People must seek wages in the cities or in Zimbabwe or South Africa or in the Ever Rest Bar," lectured Benson.

Jordan sat in silence for a few minutes. Then he spoke, "I am understanding just a little but it is confusing to me. The children can be the good thing to the life. This I know. But you, my bwanas, are saying they can be a trouble to the lives. This I cannot just be believing."

"Put it this way, Jordan. They are both. They make you happy. They work for you. They protect you when you get old. But when everyone has lots of kids, then there's a problem because the land is too little or too crowded and the economy cannot grow fast enough. So, everyone becomes a little poorer. *Mwamua* [Understand] Mr. Dama?" Benson gave it one last brief try, but his heart was not in it. Undoubtedly, he had said it all before many times.

Jordan sat in silence again. Finally he asked, "Are you having children, Bwana Kandoole?"

"Yes, I have three."

"So you are not doing this zero population, is it?"

"Well, Mr. Dama, I am an African man first, before I am an economist. So we will see." Benson smiled at me, then simply remarked, "Balaka's coming up. Let's get some more beer."

"Let's get twenty beers. One for each of Jordan's lucky children." My comment put an end to our discussion.

Chapter Seventeen

In Spite of Ourselves

"This is a hellhole, isn't it, Jordan?"

"What, my boss?"

"This damn hospital's a nightmare. And it's supposed to be one of the best in Malawi because it's got three physicians."

"Well, the Dr. Kim is too good to my Asafu. This I am knowing."

"True. But it's still a hellhole. It stinks from people's bodies, and there's garbage all over the place. You're probably better off in the village with the sing'anga."

Jordan did not respond as we continued to sit in silence on the front fenders of my small gray car, our feet resting on the bumper. The shade of a sixty-foot blue gum tree made it possible to sit this way on such a hot day, and we continued to stare at the long lines of out-patients who filled the gray front khonde of the old hospital. The Zomba Hospital was one of three general hospitals in Malawi, and presumably it was better than the small district hospitals since it had doctors, including a surgeon. Its reputation for reasonable care attracted more referrals; consequently, overcrowding had reached a scale unknown at the rural hospitals.

"This boy Asafu is too lucky, boss. The foot to this time can be almost straight."

"Let's hope so. Anyway it's better than it was two years ago. It was really a club foot then," I answered.

"This boy is a lucky one then."

"Yes, he is lucky. Dr. Kim just won't operate on club feet. And it's not that difficult an operation," I said.

"Why is this, boss?"

"Because of infection. He doesn't like to cut through the skin because so many people become infected and die. When he put Asafu asleep and then simply twisted Asafu's foot into place, I couldn't believe it. You won't believe how hard he had to twist his foot, to rip things like tendons and ligaments on one side of his ankle. Now fifteen casts later, and Asafu should be walking on the bottom at last."

"This boy stands now to the plaster and is stepping and the foot is a bit flat. True, boss."

"I noticed that yesterday when Ida brought him from Ntcheu. So, we'll see in a few minutes."

The steady line of patients was even longer now and things would probably continue this way for the remainder of the day, just like every other day. The treatment inside was a mockery to medicine, and I often wondered whether the people understood how inferior their medical care truly was. I also knew that desperate people needed to take action on their own behalf, and I remembered taking Jordan's thirteen-year-old daughter, Chimwemwe, here one night at two o'clock in a state of uncontrollable hysteria. The medical assistant gave her two green pills which were good "for this type of thing," so he claimed; and the next day Jordan sent Ida and the still hysterical Chimwemwe off on the bus to his village where the sing'anga, he claimed, would cure her. Jordan's confidence in the medical system, at least as it appeared to apply to psychological problems, was not great, and I guessed most people assessed it similarly.

"I am thanking you, my boss, for doing this for your Jordan and the little Asafu."

"What's that?"

"Thanking you for these many months of fetching Asafu and Ida and for this Dr. Kim who is doing the treatment to the foot."

"No problem. That's what friends are for, aren't they?" I spoke quickly.

"You are the best friend to Jordan in this world."

"Oh, you have better friends at home, I'm sure."

"No, boss, you are the best friend. You are my brother. This I know."

"Well, I'm happy to hear that." I turned to Jordan, smiled, and reached over and touched his shoulder. He sometimes said this type of thing to me, and I never failed to let him know that I appreciated his feelings and his willingness to voice them. As I turned forward again, I noticed Ida coming toward us with Asafu in her arms. Dr. Kim was following them.

Jordan and I stood and walked toward them. Ida and Dr. Kim had huge smiles on their faces. We greeted them quickly, and Jordan reached out to touch the foot of his son.

Jordan spoke in Chichewa to Ida, and she put Asafu down for us to judge the results of his two-year ordeal. Asafu was still unsteady, because all his standing and the little bit of walking he had managed had been performed while his foot was still in the cast. Nevertheless, he seemed delighted with himself, and his foot was flat, from front to back, although it rested noticeably on the outside edge.

Dr. Kim spoke. "It's not perfect, as you can see. But it is a big improvement, and I believe he'll be able to walk. He won't be a footballer, but he'll do fine."

Jordan listened intently. He spoke again to Ida and listened carefully to her reply. He reached down and touched the foot. He stood and stared at it. Then he picked Asafu up and hugged him and examined his foot again. He passed Asafu over to Ida.

"It is good. The boy can walk, this I can see. So it is good. This one can be too lucky. True, boss." Jordan seemed shy.

"I agree, bambo. He is lucky, because without Dr. Kim he'd be like the thousands of others we see everywhere." While my comment was so obviously small talk, it was certainly true that Asafu was one of the very lucky ones. Simple problems like club feet did not usually get treated here in Malawi.

Dr. Kim, a South Korean surgeon clearly able to function medically under very difficult circumstances, was well regarded in our little community, and as a favor to me, he had straightened the foot. Sensing Jordan's inability to thank him, he simply stepped forward and shook Jordan's hand. Jordan seemed unprepared but managed to thank him several times. Dr. Kim just wished us all good luck and departed, and the four of us got into my car for the short trip home.

"Asafu's a happy guy tonight. Look at him motor around." The seven of us who crowded into our kitchen to watch him and to share in his happiness were a little proud of ourselves for helping him.

Pleased to be the center of attention, Asafu understood that he was to keep moving and to show off his redesigned foot. Still a little unsteady, he moved along the sink to a chair and then back to Ida, who was sitting in the doorway. We clapped to show our approval, and he repeated his little journey to show us it was no fluke. This time we added laughter to our applause, and Asafu now appeared so thoroughly pleased with himself that he was about to start out on another journey when Ida pulled him to her lap.

With bedtime approaching, Claire, Ian, and Alison left. After finishing a piece of chocolate cake that Jordan had baked for dinner, Ida and Asafu departed, and I overheard Jordan tell Ida he would soon join them at the quarters. Doviko continued to wash the dishes while Jordan finished cooking some nsima for Doviko and himself. They often ate what we ate, but their favorite food was this nsima, and they cooked it almost every night.

"You want a beer with that horrible stuff, Jordan?" I asked.

"Yes, boss," Jordan laughed and Doviko smiled.

"You want a Coke or a Fanta, Doviko?"

"Yes, bwana. A Coke can do."

I went to the refrigerator and took out two beers and the Coke and removed the caps. I placed the drinks on the counter and stepped out to the khonde to listen to the radio and to wait for Jordan and Doviko.

"Boss, are these two chaps who are coming to dinner tomorrow the young schoolboys that the crazy Bastone has taken to the United States from those days to Ntcheu?" Jordan asked.

"Lester and Nelson. That's them, all right."

"And the third, boss, where is this one?"

"Rodney. He's still in the U.S. In a city called Detroit, I heard. That's what Nelson said anyway."

Jordan turned to Doviko, who was sitting on the cement, and began to tell him the story of Bastone and the three boys. As Jordan spoke, Doviko passed him a pie-shaped wedge of nsima, so the story was occasionally stopped when Jordan took a mouthful or when Doviko's exclamations made Jordan laugh. It was a long and interesting story inasmuch as it covered so many years. They had both survived beautifully and had graduated successfully from prestigious American universities, and now they were well situated in Malawi.

"Say, my boss, why was this Bastone just doing this?" Jordan's tone was serious.

"I don't know. He's a good guy. A friend, I guess."

"A friend. I can see this. He can be a too good man."

"No doubt about it. And these guys are very grateful to him. I can tell you that."

"So he is a friend to these boys? I should say these bwanas."

"Sure."

"As we are friends, boss?"

"I guess so. Except that you are employed by me, and that makes it tricky."

Jordan thought for a moment. "I am not understanding. We are not the friends? No, this cannot be." Jordan's voice trembled slightly. "No, you are Jordan's best friend to the world and my son here, Doviko, he can be telling you this to be true."

"Hold it. We're friends for sure. It's just that at the same time we're also boss and employee, bwana and bambo. You know."

"But we are still the friends, isn't it so?" Jordan looked directly at me.

"Well, of course. But first you tell me what a friend is." I found myself repeating the question I'd asked him so many years ago.

Jordan sat back in the chair and said nothing. He finished his beer, then stood and walked to the refrigerator and got himself another beer and returned.

"Maybe that's what a friend is, Bambo Jordan. You know, someone who doesn't have to ask if he can have another beer." I laughed and Doviko smiled, but Jordan was too preoccupied to be amused. "Come on, achimwene, tell me what a friend is."

"I am thinking it is just as good as a brother."

"But you don't choose a brother. And even if you don't like your brother, he is still your brother."

"So it is more special, boss?"

"I guess so. It is different, anyway. Because you choose a friend. And you can choose someone not to be your friend."

"I am seeing this, my boss."

We paused. Jordan and Doviko ate some more nsima as I tuned the radio.

Finally, I spoke. "The thing I don't know about friendship is how much one can disappoint someone else and still be a friend."

"What is this, boss?"

"Well, friends must enjoy each other and spend time together. This seems clear to me. Like we do." I hesitated. "But people are not perfect. They make mistakes, so they must disappoint their friends eventually. See?"

"I am a bit confused, my boss."

"I am saying you cannot be a perfect friend. You will disappoint your friends eventually. So I wonder how many bad things one person can do before the other doesn't like him anymore. In other words, a friendship is tricky. It is delicate and can end."

Jordan looked at me carefully and then over to Doviko. He sipped some beer and continued to eat his nsima in silence. My comments lacked specifics, but I thought he understood me well.

"I, Jordan, am your friend. Is this not so, boss?"

"Yes, you are."

"Am I disappointing my boss?"

"I just said all friends disappoint each other."

Jordan's face flushed. "How is it that I am disappointing you, my boss?"

I smiled. "There's too many ways to tell. We'd be up all night if I started my list." I laughed, alone. Doviko looked at both of us, and I knew I was not going to get out of this one easily.

"How is it that I am disappointing my boss?" Jordan pressed.

"You drink too much at the wrong time of the day. How's that, for one?"

"Yes, I am a drinker. This I can know. But I am doing my duties to the evening. This I am knowing, sure."

"Let's not argue about it. We'll be going home soon, so there's not much point discussing it now."

"Is there another, my boss?" Jordan persisted.

"Well, you're a goddamned snob."

"What is this 'snob'?"

I smiled, but Jordan was not amused. "Actually, to me you're not a snob. It's just that you think you're better than just about everyone else."

"Is this so, boss?"

"Well, isn't it?"

Jordan hesitated. "Yes, this is so, just a little bit."

"See, you don't deny it."

"Well, I am clever and handsome. This I know. So it can be like this." Jordan's answer was as amusing as it was predictable, and I shook my head and smiled. Jordan continued, "This is the only two things that I am disappointing, then?" He waited for my reply.

"How about last Christmas when you two bastards took off, and Mommy and the kids were in the States, and I was so sick I thought I'd die. You guys knew I was sick, but you were so selfish about going home that you just left me. Right?"

Jordan and Doviko froze.

Their thoughtlessness had provoked me to scold them, bitterly and severely. I accused them of extreme selfishness at a time when I legitimately needed them, at a time, ironically, when I had generously given them gifts, extra cash, and extra vacation days. To be sure, our friendship weathered this episode, but my disappointment in their behavior was keen. Obviously, they had no answer, and I knew they would make no further comments.

"So do you want me to go on, bambo?"

Jordan rubbed his face and thought and then glanced at Doviko. "No, I am disappointing you this I can see. Is this not so, my son?" Doviko nodded, his eyes lowered.

The three of us spoke no more. Again I played with the radio, and they finished eating. Doviko took the dishes into the kitchen and began washing them.

"Say, Jordan. How have I disappointed you?"

"No, my boss. You are a too good man to your Jordan and to my son here. You cannot be disappointing."

"Not true, my friend. I had to disappoint you sometime. Friends do that. So tell me."

"No, boss. There is no disappointing to us."

"Come on, Jordan, tell me. Maybe I didn't pay you enough."

"No, you have been generous to your Jordan and Doviko here. It is a little all right."

I smiled, but I pressed. "Come on, you can think of something."

Jordan hesitated and he looked a little nervous. Finally he said, "It is the driving, my boss."

"You mean when I wouldn't let Kanama finish the driving lessons."

"This is it, my boss."

"I understand. But you really angered me that day when I told both of you not to drive on Naisi Road because you weren't ready. Kanama knew better, and so did you."

"I can be understanding the boss," Jordan spoke quietly. "But if Jordan was having the license, I could be a driver as Mr. Kanama and not just the cook. It can be the chance for this too good job."

Now it was my turn to be silent. I knew Jordan thought that a license would be his key to improved employment, even though Kanama felt Jordan was too old to become a skillful lorry driver or a chauffeur. Nevertheless, my annoyance at their not following my instructions when Jordan was taking lessons led me to deny him the use of my car. As a result, Jordan did not get his driver's license. Clearly, I had disappointed Jordan, deeply disappointed him.

We sat without speaking. Doviko came back and joined us.

"Get Jordan and me another beer, will you, Doviko?" I broke the silence.

"No, my boss. I am not wanting the beer. I must be resting. My Ida she can be waiting to the quarters."

Doviko stopped and looked at me. "OK. Skip the beers."

"You are not wishing the beer?" Doviko asked.

"No, we're both going to go to bed." Jordan and I both stood up.

"Well, good night, boss."

"Good night, my friend." I started inside but stopped. "Achimwene."

"Yes, boss?"

"So, we're still friends even if we disappointed each other. Right?"

"Yes, we are still the friends, my boss. It can be this way until the death."

"Great. That's the way I see it too. Good night."

"Good night, boss."

Chapter Eighteen

Farewell Prizes

I set the last suitcase down near the dining-room door beside the other four and the assortment of small bags we would carry onto the plane. Jordan and Doviko had already moved out of their quarters, and the electricity and water had been shut off. We were waiting for Kanama, who would collect me and the luggage, and then we would pick up Claire and the kids at the Government Hotel, where we had spent the last two nights. Jordan would ride along to the airport with us, and that evening both he and Doviko would begin working in new positions. Doviko's cooking skills had improved dramatically under Jordan's tutelage, and he was going to be a combination cook and houseboy for a young, single English woman, a librarian at the university. Jordan would work for an English couple with two children. Amazingly, it was the man who had lived with us years before in Ntcheu when he served as a British volunteer, and he had taught in the secondary school there with the old gang.

I tried to make small talk about how quickly two years had passed. Jordan and Doviko appeared quite strained about our departure. Even though they had known from the beginning that this day would come, it did not make it easier for them. And the prospect of new employers, with all the trials and adjustments that that would mean, added to the strain.

"My son here and I, Jordan, are just thanking you for the goodness of the two years. Is this not so, my son?" Jordan's face was flushed.

"Yes," Doviko spoke very softly.

"Speak up, my son, the boss must be hearing you. You cannot

185

just be so quiet.''

Doviko was embarrassed but as he always had done, he followed orders. ''Yes, I am very much thanking you and Mommy for the kindness and for the two months of the money of which you are giving.''

''You guys are both welcome. You deserve it. Just don't waste it. You've both got jobs already, so you can do something useful.'' They had thanked me several times, and I knew they were sincere. ''I hope you got enough shirts and pots and pans and blankets yesterday.''

''Yes, bwana. We are too lucky for the goods,'' Jordan spoke for them both.

''Good, my friends. I'm happy if you're happy.''

We spoke no more. Jordan stepped over to the dining room window and looked down on the beautiful road wound up along the mountainside from the center of town. ''Mr. Kanama is coming. My son, we must be taking the katundu now,'' Jordan called out.

Doviko stepped forward and grabbed two of the large suitcases, and I took the remaining two.

''I can carry, my boss,'' Jordan said.

''No, you just check the house again to make sure we've got everything.''

Doviko and I were quickly down the stairs to the top of the driveway as Kanama turned off the main road.

''Boss.''

''Yes, Doviko?''

''Can you be giving the football shoes to this case?''

''You want the new soccer shoes?'' I was surprised by Doviko's courage.

''Yes, bwana,'' Doviko spoke softly.

I hesitated. ''I guess so. Well, OK. Yes, sure. Take them if you like.''

Doviko turned the case on its side, and I bent over and unzipped it. He located the shoes quickly. Then I zipped up the suitcase and stood it up as Kanama pulled to a stop.

''Doviko, hide those shoes in the garage and come back later and get them.'' Feeling that I had been generous enough, I said, ''Let's keep this between us.'' Doviko stepped into the garage, and I went up the stairs to the house to get the remainder of our luggage.

''Boss.''

''Yes, Jordan.''

''I was just wondering a little bit if it can be possible that my bwana can be giving me this fine radio of which we have been enjoying together for such a time.''

I hesitated and smiled, knowing Jordan had not changed in all these years. "I don't know, Jordan. I promised it to Ian. He likes to listen to the radio now. So, no. I am going to keep it." I reached down and grabbed two small pieces of hand luggage, one of which contained the radio. "Let's hurry. We should get to the airport in about two hours."

We stepped outside. Doviko joined us, and I passed him the luggage. I turned and locked the door.

"Jordan, take the key. After you and Kanama come back from the airport, take it to the university housing office. Kanama knows where."

"OK, boss."

The three of us stood still a moment. We looked at each other awkwardly.

I spoke. "It was a great two years in this house. We had a lot of fun, didn't we?"

Jordan and Doviko nodded their heads but did not smile.

"Come on, guys. Claire and the kids are waiting." I started toward the driveway.

"Boss."

"What, Jordan?"

"Can you be coming back to Malawi?"

I smiled. "I sure hope so. I'm planning on it." I continued on.

"Did you hear the boss, my son? He can be with us again to Malawi."

Top: *Nelson, Bruce, and Jordan in Zomba, 1981.* Bottom: *Jordan and our dog, 1964.*

Afterword

Robert, Lester, Paxton, Makwangwala, and Misomali all died in the late 1960s. Doviko and Kanama are living in Zomba; Ben and Benson are still at the University of Malawi, and Ian is a businessman in Blantyre. The schoolboy Lester is a biologist with a Ph.D., and Nelson is a journalist. Both live in Malawi. I regret I have lost track of Mbepula and Chumia. Dave Bush died in Vietnam after his service in Malawi, but all the other Peace Corps volunteers are alive and well and living throughout the United States.

Some words change from the early part of the narrative to the later period, e.g., pounds to kwacha, Rhodesia to Zimbabwe, but these changes should cause the reader little difficulty. In addition, there is a debate among linguists about the spelling of some Chichewa words. While there is no easy solution to this problem, I have been influenced by Gregory Orr's and Carol Myers Scotton's 1982 handbook, *Learning Chichewa*, Michigan State University, Language Series, East Lansing.

Special thanks to my friend and colleague Dr. Carroll Grimes. Her generosity, as always, was boundless.